*To my dear friends
Tony
&
Irene
Fournier*

Waterline

*A Discussion of Education, Society,
and their Mutual Interaction*

*With sincere thanks
for 25+ years of
love & friendship*

DANIEL HELM

Daniel Helm

WestBow
PRESS
A DIVISION OF THOMAS NELSON

Copyright © 2013 Daniel Helm.

All rights reserved. No part of this book may be used or reproduced by any means, graphic, electronic, or mechanical, including photocopying, recording, taping or by any information storage retrieval system without the written permission of the publisher except in the case of brief quotations embodied in critical articles and reviews.

WestBow Press books may be ordered through booksellers or by contacting:

WestBow Press
A Division of Thomas Nelson
1663 Liberty Drive
Bloomington, IN 47403
www.westbowpress.com
1 (866) 928-1240

Because of the dynamic nature of the Internet, any web addresses or links contained in this book may have changed since publication and may no longer be valid. The views expressed in this work are solely those of the author and do not necessarily reflect the views of the publisher, and the publisher hereby disclaims any responsibility for them.

Any people depicted in stock imagery provided by Thinkstock are models, and such images are being used for illustrative purposes only. Certain stock imagery © Thinkstock.

ISBN: 978-1-4908-0995-3 (sc)
ISBN: 978-1-4908-0996-0 (e)

Library of Congress Control Number: 2013917450

Printed in the United States of America.

WestBow Press rev. date: 10/11/2013

Table of Contents

Acknowledgements ix
Chapter 1:   The Waterline 1
Chapter 2:   Choosing a Profession 16
Chapter 3:   Cultural Influences 29
Chapter 4:   Uneducated educators? 50
Chapter 5:   Science and Society 65
Chapter 6:   Around the Horn 81
Chapter 7:   Special Education, a Growing Concern 100
Chapter 8:   Sex Education in a Modern Gomorrah 107
Chapter 9:   Coaching and Extracurricular Activities 130
Chapter 10: Focus on the Students 140
Chapter 11: Working with Parents 157
Chapter 12: Working with Administrators 163
Chapter 13: Education, Politics and Unions 175
Chapter 14: Reasons for Optimism 196
Chapter 15: Wish List 203
Chapter 16: Final Thoughts 209
Index 213

DEDICATION

To my wife Kana
and my girls
Sakura, Hannah and Karen.
With all of my Love

Acknowledgements

To the good friends who guided me while writing this book with their kindness and valuable advice, my most sincere thanks. To Dave Cornell who told me that whether or not I thought science was the most important discipline, I had better straighten up on my grammar if I wanted to publish a book. Thank you to a friend and fellow teacher who guided me in improving my grammar and provided great encouragement. Despite the best efforts of others, I am sure I still messed up enough grammar to make English teachers cringe, maybe not Jenna Warner, but less compassionate English teachers will, perhaps, not be so gentle in their corrections. Thank you to Jan Price, who inspired the first complete rewrite of this book with her invaluable insight. I am grateful not only for the time you took to read the book, but the time you spent clearly articulating where improvements were needed and why. To Chris Cioffi who understood that a book's message is not going to be palatable without a balanced discourse. Thank you to Justin Kiefer who provided not only opinions from our upcoming generation, but the in-depth analysis of a professional. To Anthony DeBlasi, who has been family, friend and inspiration, thank you for giving a construction worker turned teacher the feedback of an elite scholar

Thank you to Mary Lanni who gave me my first job in education. Thank you to my parents and family, who have always been a source of joy and inspiration. Thank you to the great friends I have had throughout life: The MNHS group, may we always have good times together, my Kean College friends, the men and women who kept me sane on the Polar Star while peeling potatoes, chipping paint, and working mess duty. Finally, thank you to my professors at ESU who not only gave me a great education, but who welcomed me back as an adjunct.

CHAPTER ONE

The Waterline

During the age of wooden hulled sailing ships, a ship in battle hoped for a chance to put a cannon ball in the waterline of the enemy ship. This was difficult to do, so typically, a navy captain would have his men fire at the rigging. This would disable the vessel, then his crew could board it and fight with musket and cutlass. When the waves were sufficiently high, an enemy's ship might rise in the water in relation to your ship. This would allow a well timed shot from the cannon deck to pierce the opponent's waterline, sinking the vessel with ease.

In a culture, the children represent the waterline. Destroy the children and you destroy the culture. Our children are currently under attack from several directions and need our help and protection. To that end, it is fair to say that teaching is one of the most rewarding careers a person could pursue. Teaching is a valuable profession, but I have great concern for the industry called "education". Its substance is the honorable task of giving knowledge and opportunities to the next generation, yet it is infected with waste, discord and mediocrity.

This is a hard statement to make, yet one which if not made, leaves us without the correct diagnosis to correct the problems we are facing. When states compete to see which one provides the best education, we see states comparing which is closest to achieving a 50% rating in having students read at grade level. That is not a judgment on which state is most successful, but rather, which state is the least ineffective. In any tax payer funded endeavor, there is no profit, thus insufficient incentive to achieve excellence. This makes education a quagmire of earnest and insincere motives. There are teachers who work tirelessly to help students learn, and there are teachers who merely go through the motions. There are school districts which raise the level of achievement through effort and commitment to children, and there are school districts which create a false impression of improvement by cheating on standardized tests.

Changes in this country over the past few decades have created new and frightening crises to address. During refresher training, sailors learn how to repair and patch damaged ships until they can be taken into dry dock for a complete overhaul. While a ship is underway, "shoring up" damaged bulkheads allows the ship to continue on course. Our country needs not only to have the bulkheads of education shored up, we need to change course. If a ship is heading east and wants to go north, there is a need to change direction, but heading west just to have changed direction does no one any good. As a teacher, my experience has shown that doing the best possible job for children requires not only the effort to educate them, but the ability to navigate the minefields of union intrigue, administrators' ambitions, and all of the cultural changes that have impacted the mindset of our youth. Writing this book is an affirmation that the ship of public education does not need to be scuttled; it is a serviceable ship, but it has suffered damage.

Navigating the minefields within the waterways of education is one approach to enjoying a long career. I disagree with the idea of avoiding the mines. Education would improve if the waterways were cleared of the mines.

Fixing education will not fix America, but it can help to put America back on the right track. At the very least, it could stop us from adding to the problems of our culture. Improving education requires practical solutions. The conventional wisdom of educators is, too often, the product of a mindset, with insufficient experience outside of classrooms. Obtaining a diverse background prior to entering education will influence a person's approach to class room management, presentation of information and assignment of priorities. For people who went to high school, then went to college, then at the age of 22 began a career where they were the experts, and they were to be listened to at all times by a group of young people who were unequal to the adult's expertise, there is a risk of losing the ability to listen and learn, and work laterally with others. There may be a detachment from what it takes to succeed outside of the classroom, to succeed in the "real world".

This is not to say that success in the class room for a person from any other professional background is a given, or even possible. I have seen people who've been successful professionals in other fields lack the ability to run a class room properly. Teaching is an art, in that it cannot be done from a cookbook, and one solution does not always fix the same problem on two different days. There is simply a type of person who becomes a great teacher and many people who are more capable of success in other endeavors. One simple and accurate description of what it takes to be a great teacher comes from H.L. Mencken when he says: "A man who knows a subject so thoroughly, a man so soaked in it that he eats it, sleeps it and dreams it—this man can always teach it with success, no matter how little he knows of technical pedagogy".

That "love of a subject" is not the focus of education for educators; rather education for educators is focused on the technical pedagogy. As a result, we teachers know how to process children through the system, but we do not always engender in them a love for what they have learned. The most successful teachers radiate a love of knowledge. When a child graduates high school, they may be truly prepared for advanced learning, or they may have simply been advanced as a way of avoiding the effort necessary to educate them. Teachers who have worked in a field for which they are training students will usually be better than an otherwise equal candidate who only knows how to teach, but who has never employed the technical skills of their discipline as a means of making a living. I know a woodshop teacher whose students create showroom quality furniture; I believe it is due to his success in that field before entering a classroom. A person who knows how to learn is always a better teacher than a person who has been taught how to teach. Conversely, when an instructor has only practical experience, his or her ability to present it many be insufficient, or their commitment to a deep breadth of knowledge on the topic may be sacrificed to an expediency borne of a willingness to take the shortcuts which may be common when working in the field. Learning how to present information is important and can not be ignored when preparing teachers for the profession, but the time devoted to pedagogy should be significantly less than the time spent learning the actual discipline the teacher will teach.

Education is the career which touches the next generation. Protecting and nurturing the next generation falls on the shoulders of all adults, but not to the extent that it falls on the shoulders of educators, who are second only to parents and close family in carrying that honorable burden. It is the most worthwhile burden a person can carry. This book is for future educators, for concerned adults, and for the younger generation who will perhaps have a chance to consider view points they had not before analyzed.

Steve Jobs credits his having once been fired from a job with giving him the motivation to achieve greatness in his field. Many teachers have never experienced the angst of concerning themselves with their employment. Year after year, decade after decade, they know their job is just sitting there waiting for them. The opportunity to touch the lives of the next generation motivates some teachers to drive themselves to be the best they can be. Other teachers seem not to consider what a great opportunity they are holding. They just enjoy sitting on that security. For me, the year I quit the teachers' union was a year of endless trials dealing with ridiculous attacks and petty nonsense. It was the year I realized the extent to which some people in schools are willing to destroy kids' educations to serve their own motives. That year,

I needed to decide if I wanted to leave education or redouble my efforts to improve it. This book is my response.

This school will never tolerate more than mediocrity, so don't try is one statement I heard, which has greatly motivated me in writing this book. It is not merely the comment, but the pseudo-wisdom behind the comment; many young teachers are advised to learn a school's culture, and then fit in as a way of finding job security. A young adult who learns that a school will never tolerate more than mediocrity and then blends into that mindset has lost his or her chance to ever be an agent for change. Moreover, such a teacher will never seek to fully develop into more than the accepted norm. Young people need to enter education with the desire to improve it if they are to serve it well. If they do not, they may easily be influenced by factors beyond their control. Most teachers I've spoken with have experienced administrators lacking the where-with-all to properly lead a school and yet carry themselves with the overbearing aplomb of a Napoleon. Many teachers have known adults who lack the work ethic to keep a minimum wage job through their first shift, and yet make statements such as: I run the union, and I run this school. Those are attitudes which could be corrected if members of that first group, those teachers who are capable of being more than mediocre, resisted the temptation to accept mediocrity from themselves and others. Schools need people willing to say that they will give their absolute best effort for their students. When such people stand up and demand more of themselves on behalf of children, schools need administrators who will not allow such people to be beaten down.

A video became popular in the spring of 2013 in which a student virtually pleads with his teacher to reach out to the students and help them learn. Our culture leaves much to be desired, but the desire for improvement is there. The boy in that video wanted to learn, his teacher was earning a paycheck. Feeding his desire to learn is the reason for the paycheck.

If the environment in which our children are being raised is to improve, the improvement of the culture must come from the parents who must decide with greater moral clarity the influences to which their children will be exposed, and the teachers who must better equip children to succeed outside of the classroom and throughout their lives. Responsibility for the welfare of American children must fall on the shoulders of not only these two groups of people, but by extension onto the shoulders of industry and media who must come to learn via economic pressures that it is expected and demanded that they provide to children wholesome, enriching products. If a young man like Angus T. Jones can bravely speak out against his own bread and butter once he reaches an age where he realizes the effect of media on society, those who care the most about children should be the driving force in moving our culture in a positive direction; teachers and parents should not be passengers accepting the lead of others.

Whether a child's home life or their school life, or their social ties have the biggest impact on their maturation will vary from child to child. This book will focus on school life more than the other two, while acknowledging the reality that all three are impacted by the health of a society. In a healthy society, people can achieve or fail according to their own efforts, but their failures can be overcome when people seek the best from themselves and treat others with dignity and kindness.

Having taught in both public and private schools, I've seen two worlds. There are comparisons to be made which could benefit both types of institutions. Many educators came from public school settings, then directly entered public school teaching after college. Having seen what private school children receive in terms of their education, I try to mimic that for my public school children. It is not the children who vary in the two settings, it is the expectations. Offering public school children a private school education can be problematic in public schools, as some union leaders try to regulate the efforts of other teachers. What may have started as a way of providing job security to less capable teachers often ends up being a way to make mediocrity shine through the destruction of excellence. Trying to be the very best you can be in a public school does not necessarily endear a teacher to their union. Once a culture of complacency reigns it becomes generational, and each new group of teachers is exposed to a status quo which should never have been accepted.

Fighting complacency takes encouragement. Encouragement may come from parents sending in a jar of homemade jam, or from some homemade scones, or even a coworker's willingness to be unpopular in order to be noble and confront a commonly accepted practice which is wrong.

There was an episode of Little House on the Prairie featuring Mr. Edwards, who, while babysitting the Ingalls girls cleaned the dishes by having the dog lick the plates. Thankfully, those girls knew enough to sneak down in the middle of the night and actually wash the plates. Had they been raised by Mr. Edwards, I am sure they would have thought that a plate licked by a dog was clean enough. To believe that the pursuit of excellence is the norm, students need to be exposed to it. "Normal" can be defined as whatever situation people have been exposed to most frequently.

In assessing public education, consider the death of baseball's Billy Martin. Billy Martin had the most brilliant baseball mind of this generation; he was also famous for his bellicose nature and tenacity. He died by driving his car into a drainage ditch. According to *High, Wild and Tight* (Golenbock, 1994, pg 473) as he swerved off of the road he gunned the gas pedal, and tried to swerve back onto the road, causing the wreck. If instead, he had slammed on his brakes, and then gotten help from a tow truck driver, he would have lived. Insisting on going in the direction we are going is not the solution. The status quo is keeping a lot of administrators secure and well paid, and for many teachers, the atmosphere lends itself to stagnation. It is not time for us to gun the gas and keep going in the direction we have been going. It is time for education to slam on the brakes, and ask for help. Of course, it is easier for a small vehicle to change directions more efficiently than a large vehicle. By mandating federal standards, we choose to drive the biggest vehicle possible. If individual states chose their own standards, eventually, some would rise to the top, providing incentive for other states to follow. 1,500 students every year earn doctorates in education. Word would manage to get around as to which states were most successful via analysis of the data. States could then adjust another state's techniques to their own set of circumstances.

If the federal government is to be involved in education, they should take a softer approach, leaving a great deal of authority in the hands of local districts. They should work with states, and endeavor to avoid layering one bureaucracy on top of another. Approaches to the same problem will be different in different areas, and local boards of education need to be able to adjust to their own set of circumstances.

When people talk about changing the nature of education, they will often discuss how similar education is today to what it was one hundred years ago: You walk into a room, see rows of chairs, a teacher lecturing, students taking notes, and there seems to be no improvement since the industrial revolution. Well, unless the future image of a class room was to be little tykes flying around on hover crafts while completing calculus problems mentally in their gigantic heads which evolved to resemble gourds the size of watermelons, it is not so bad that students sit in chairs and learn from their teachers (as long as they are learning). There should however be no question that certain facets have changed, and needed to change, but you can still learn literature by reading a book, and you can still learn what a cell looks like by using a microscope. Not everything needs to change as times change. In some schools, the local school district is, to some degree, a jobs program, with many people returning to the school where they grew up. If that school has, and had, low standards, the new employees will merely transmit the culture of complacency to the next generation. It is not always a bad thing that young people return to the school where they grew up. Right now, there are students in my class who I know will, without doubt, become tremendous teachers. The problem lies in situations where connections bring into the district employees who were of a lower quality than competing candidates with superior skills, but inferior connections. While there is a certain amount of: It's not what you know, but who you know in industry, education must be exactly the opposite. It must be about what you know. If people in industry choose to make inferior choices in their hiring practices through cronyism, eventually, the free market will serve as an agent of correction. Schools are spending the tax money of other people; there is no market competition to cause a correction, but there should be. If I could, within my own school district, assemble a team including one teacher for each discipline, and one special education teacher, we could provide at least a portion of the students with the best possible education. Independently functioning "academies" within larger schools would create competition. Retired baseball star Graig Nettles, in his book *Balls,* explained that once he learned that the organization he was playing with did not have the same drive to win that he had, his focus became trying to attract the eye of another club's general manager. Competition is good.

Some schools are excellent in what they do. School communities are highly individualized and no amount of federal programming will ever force all schools into a cookie cutter mold. In fact, the more we try to breed uniformity in schools, the closer we come to the lowest common denominator, as excellence can never be uniformly mandated, but mediocrity can result from too much homogenization of expectations. Schools have some phenomenal educators and administrators, and schools have people who could never stay employed without tenure. The more of the former that schools attract and retain, the better their product will be.

Politicians are expected to solve problems. When Jimmy Carter created the Department of Education on October 17th, 1979, he created another layer of government bureaucracy. It has not to date shown itself to be the solution to problems in education. It does however provide more jobs to people who are in the field of education and who do not have direct contact with students. Problems are always best solved by individuals with passion rather than bureaucracies.

Education's product is not the child; educators do not deal in a world of products. In education, the knowledge that the child has amassed during the educator's brief interlude into their life may be considered a form of a product. If so, it is a product which can not be recalled and later corrected, like faulty brake lights on a new car. It is a once and done product. It is one which must not be carelessly provided.

To merely create in children a will to learn is insufficient. At times in my life when I was digging ditches, if a foreman had come to me at the end of a shift and I had not moved one shovel full of dirt, but I explained that I did have the will to dig, I would have been fired, and my boss would have done no better in explaining to his boss that he had engendered in me a desire to dig ditches. Helping a child "want to learn" is meaningless unless that student then actually learns something.

While educating children, teachers should also be mindful of the students' emotional well being. However, the emotional welfare of the child is a secondary goal in education. It should be the primary goal of the family to provide that piece of the puzzle.

Educators should do nothing to diminish what has been done at home. Rather, they should reinforce all of the positive lessons parents have provided, and when necessary instill confidence and a sense of self worth in the children whose home life leaves them prone to emotional scarring, confusion and the dangers of making poor choices. Children may feel a sense of despair regarding issues which are beyond their control during youth, so they need to know that they will be able to control many of those issues when they are running their own lives. The purpose of public education is to give them that opportunity.

As the number of families with some form of impairment have increased, whether due to social engineering or loss of personal responsibility, the amount of time schools are mandated to spend on emotional welfare programs has significantly increased, causing a loss of instructional time, thus a less competitive workforce. Quite simply, if the entire school is attending an assembly instructing students not to use social media in abusive ways, they are not in class learning about math, science literature and history. Moreover, and this is a personal observation, the teachers whose lives are the most together come to school to teach their lessons. Teachers whose own lives are chaos always seem to be the ones ignoring the curriculum and hanging out giving the kids "life lessons" instead of teaching their academic subjects to the children.

Rather than trying to find better ways to repair the damage done to our culture's waterline, we need to disarm the enemy ships. At the very least, we need to keep our children out of range. Friends of mine once complained that while watching a G-Rated movie on TV with their small children the show was interrupted by a condom commercial from the company sponsoring the program. It is clear that our children are in range of pernicious influences, and we need to protect their innocence.

While countering cultural influences becomes increasingly necessary for educators, schools should be primarily focused on

Waterline

the transfer of knowledge. The obvious pathway of knowledge in education is to be from teacher to student. Yet, it is not impossible to receive knowledge and wisdom from those who are younger than we are, and teachers need to be willing to listen to students. Consider an essay penned by Alexander Hamilton on December 15th, 1774. Depending on which date of his birth you accept (there are two debated years: 1757 or 1755) he was either 19 or 17 when he wrote the following:

"Were not the disadvantages of slavery too obvious to stand in need of it, I might enumerate and describe the tedious train of calamities inseparable from it. I might show that it is fatal to religion and morality; that it tends to debase the mind, and corrupt its noblest springs of action. I might show that it relaxes the sinews of industry, clips the wings of commerce, and introduces misery and indigence of every kind."

Yes, a teenager can write with such ability. A teenager can also communicate via an endless stream of LOL, CUL8R and JK short hand. The human mind merely needs proper training. If schools choose the abnegation of that duty through willful indifference or misguided implementation of ineffectual curricula, the students will then be left to fend for themselves with little direction as to how they may obtain knowledge, or how best to pursue the advancement of their own intellectual abilities.

So, how is it that a teenager like Alexander could have written so well over two centuries ago? He never had the opportunity to cut and paste large tracts of internet content into an essay he would hand in, so instead, he sharpened his mind to a piercing point. Our technology has made information easier to obtain and present, but without first processing that information intellectually, the student is merely a conveyor belt of information from a research source to a teacher for grading, then they move on having not fully infused that knowledge into their own psyche. In the type of classical education our founding fathers received, a student would stand before his or her classmates and recite from memory. They would not put out a tri-fold and read the words they had cut and pasted from a website.

A strong education decreases the likelihood that a person will absorb misinformation easily. As "news" programming has increasingly become partisan, it is interesting to watch how the same story will be presented with two completely different spins on the same day, but on two different networks. Take any story involving a decision that a politician has made, then choose one of two prefaces for you story: Choice One: "In a brilliant move…" versus Choice Two "Adding another blunder to his resume…" Regardless of what fact you insert next, the audience has already had their opinion formed by the context in which the basic fact (soon to follow) has already been framed.

Students can best attain a thorough knowledge of the subjects they study if their teachers have a thorough knowledge of the subjects. The Socratic method of teaching requires that a student possess the ability to make proper responses to open ended questions, and the teacher possess the ability to shoot from the hip with questions. There are methods that best illustrate a student's knowledge base, and they require teachers with a thorough knowledge of the subject they teach. In strengthening young people's minds, those young people become less susceptible to the manipulations of others, and better able to see through the misrepresentation of facts.

Considering our mental development, we can contrast that to how we in America consider our physical development. We have a much greater focus on our physical appearance than our mental acuity. If there were two fitness trainers, and one would give her clients grades of A or B+ for eating ice cream and cheeseburgers, while her competitor insisted on 30 minutes of cardio per day, 30 minutes of weight training per day, and 15 minutes of stretching per day, we could easily see the differences in the results, and we would ignore the fact that the first trainer had students who were all on the "fitness honor roll". Results should be more important than awards. The grades would be meaningless as the true measure of success would be clear in the fitness levels of the clients of trainer two. An "A" average in a class without a solid knowledge base is meaningless.

Mental ability is different than physical fitness, and it is harder to illustrate. If an abuser of steroids likes to go shirtless, and show off his wash board abdomen, the fruits of his labors are evident. He may even be given a multimillion dollar contract for a reality TV program. If a person were to show off his mental abilities, say by hanging out at Venice Beach and calculating outputs of various calculus functions, it is very likely that someone with wash board abs would soundly pummel that mathematician.

We believe the grades passed out by teachers truly reflect the mental fitness level of the students but that may not always be the case. Ask an advanced placement history student to name the first ten presidents in order. If they stop after five, and one of the names mentioned was Ben Franklin, don't be shy about using the certificate of award they received for making the honor roll as a coffee cup coaster.

Protecting a culture's waterline is an abstract notion, it is easier to just care about kids, doing so requires being attentive to what is happening in our culture, and when necessary fighting against what is wrong. That is easier said than done because the people filling our culture with harmful values are often skilled sophists.

CHAPTER TWO

Choosing a Profession

"It is the supreme art of the teacher to awaken joy in creative expression and knowledge."

~ Albert Einstein

I love being a teacher, but am deeply disturbed by realities in the profession. My experiences, coupled with observations of other teachers with whom I've spoken indicate that some of the driving forces in education are administrators' desires to be well paid, the unions' desires to have control, and some teachers love of early dismissals and summer vacations. Genuinely caring about kids is welcome and it is common, but unfortunately when push comes to shove, it is often placed behind those motives previously mentioned. Within that tempest of ulterior motives lies a vast army of people who truly care about children. Caring about and liking kids is not enough. For a person who refuses to thoroughly learn their craft, merely saying that they truly care about children is insufficient. Any teacher who truly cares about children will demand of themselves excellence in the field. The washout rate of teachers exceeds that of any other profession. Lisa Lambert of the Washington Post wrote the following on 5/9/2006: "According to a new study from the National Education Association, a teachers union, half of new U.S. teachers are likely to quit within the first five years because of poor working conditions and low salaries." The question of utmost importance when that washout rate is considered is: How many of those washouts truly loved education and kids, and thoroughly knew their subject, but could not navigate the political environments of schools?

In that public education is a tax payer funded system, and considered essential to our way of life, it becomes taken for granted that it will always be supported. This raises the question for the professionals in the system: Is it more important to seek to be excellent in this profession, or to merely perpetuate the system while continuing to process children through the system? If a student with an A average in history can only name 5 presidents, (out of order) while believing that Benjamin Franklin was one, are we to consider the child "educated" or "processed through the system"?

I once left teaching after working in private schools for three years. My salary had been $8,000 per year in a Catholic school, then $22,000 per year in an expensive prep school; I struggled to live on such salaries, and was fighting disillusionment. During the following year, I took a graduate class and spent time working as a scientist through a temp agency. Lab work is great for a certain type of science geek, and via a temp agency a person can experience a variety of settings: working as a chemical compounder, or in quality assurance, or in microbiology, etc. It is a nice working environment, having a full lunch hour with nothing to do except kick back, working only with adults and leaving all my responsibility at the door when I left at the end of a shift.

Working only with adults is enjoyable in not having the added pressure of serving as a role model. A teacher's work ethic should be commendable, as should be their personal lives, conduct and temperament. While teachers are not public figures in the sense of professional athletes, they are, within the small community of a school, a visible representation of what it is to be an adult. Despite greatly enjoying life as a scientist, there are reasons for being a teacher which differ from the motives associated with retaining a job in industry.

Education is one of those professions where an employee in any capacity can feel they are truly filling a calling. It is a calling that can be answered daily, while other callings happen only when extreme circumstances become manifest. Joshua Lawrence Chamberlain, the hero of Little Round Top during the Battle of Gettysburg made the following comments about the Civil War: "We fight for all the guaranties of what men should love, for the protection and permanence and peace of what is most dear and sacred to every heart. That is what I am fighting for at any rate, and I could not live or die in a better cause." It is a heartfelt presentation of a noble motive. Joshua Chamberlain was also a professor; he lived a life where in war or in peace, he committed himself to noble callings. That quote was taken from a letter written by Chamberlain which was published in the June 2012 issue of Civil War Times.

[On a tangential aside, it was striking how he ended the letter which contained that quote. He ended the letter: "write me often". It made me remember my time in the service, and how mail call was a wonderful thing. The letters sailors received, we would save, and often reread. The way he closed his letter is immaterial to the thesis of this book; however, I mention the closing of his letter just in case any readers have loved ones serving in the military. If so, write them often.]

What we learn from Chamberlain is to accept the challenges of serving the callings in our lives. Teaching is not a glamorous calling, but neither is working as a custodian. Yet, in education, a conscientious custodian not only is a courteous face to the children, but also the person who makes the school's physical environment a pleasant place to be. A friend of mine who works as a custodian once saved a child's life by performing the Heimlich maneuver when the child began to choke during lunch.

Professions that leave a man or woman with calloused hands are professions where respect is easily given. Any man or woman willing to work hard to care for their child surely represents the epitome of parenthood. Lou Gehrig adored his mother, who lugged pails of water and mountains of dirty clothes up the stairs in their small New York City apartment to run her laundry business when he was growing up. Likewise, any child raised by a parent who accepted the toughest of professions as a means of giving their child a promising future is a child who has been blessed with the greatest of role models.

Motivation

Education is a noble calling, but is it a wise career choice? It is not a wise career choice if a $10,000 bonus is something you would prefer over a bagel left in the faculty room during teacher appreciation week. Being a hard working teacher involves watching some colleagues leave every day at 2:30 after investing 6 indifferent hours into their profession. It is difficult to watch the indifference of some coworkers because teachers are all grouped together. When reports come out about drop-out rates or cheating scandals involving standardized tests it is the entire profession that gets a black eye. I am one of those people who can not really tell the difference between an amazing glass of wine, and a glass of wine from a box. Most people cannot tell the difference between a great teacher and someone going through the motions. Perhaps boxed wines need a union to demand that they be priced as being of equal value with Saxum.

Education is of course, not like wine. Parents do not shop for teachers for their children. Parents enroll their children in a school and those children will either be assigned a teacher with the quality of a boxed wine or the quality of Saxum.

Teaching is a full time job, but since teachers have summers off, it is interesting to work as a temporary employee in July and August and taste different professions. Also, for teachers who are the primary bread winners of their family, ten months of paychecks do not cover 12 months of bills.

During one temporary summer assignment, I was working at the Deer Park water bottling plant in Fogelsville, Pennsylvania. A manager was having a meeting and commented that every employee was motivated to make Deer Park the best bottled water on the market. To that, one of the machine mechanics succinctly responded to his neighbor: "Bull". It was a very humorous vignette of life in the work world. The man who uttered that quote was one of your typical, put in a good shift, and then gets the heck out of there, workers. The reality is that most people go to work every day to pay the bills. They want to take care of their families, have a little left over for some savings, some recreation, etc. Working for the paycheck rather than to make the world's best bottled water is certainly not a bad mind set; particularly when compared with people who want material things, but will not put in an honest shift.

Work has its place, but it is not the be all and end all of life. Every day we have the company of friends and family to enjoy, perhaps a beautiful sunset or gentle breeze to remind us of the beauty of nature. Things do not always have to be deep and profound. Many times I envy the simplicity and joy of my dog's life. Of course, his hygiene regimen reminds me that I am actually glad to be human.

At the end of the day, the reason those mechanics at the water bottling plant are easy to respect is because they put in an honest day's work. They take care of themselves and their families. The product they produce is worthwhile, if not dramatic and they are contributing to society. Just getting up and going to work does not mean a person is doing something worthwhile or even neutral. Some people engage themselves in activities which diminish the quality of life for others. Those people need to simply assess how they are living, and make an adjustment. Of course, telling a drug dealer with a roll of $100 bills in his pocket to go back to school and learn an honest trade can be easier said than done. The fact that it is not easily done, does not change the reality that when a thirteen year old with $30,000 worth of heroin in his bedroom is shot dead, it should have been done.

Jobs do one of three things: some make the world a better place, some have little or no effect on it, and the third group makes it worse. It would be great if only the first two existed. Being an educator falls into the first category. If a teacher really cares about doing a good job, he or she will give something to the children in his or her class every day, hopefully several things. To give them knowledge, a sense of purpose, self esteem, skills and a caring environment is to give them a future. The self serving members of our society like to say that the reason to care about young people is because they will care about us when we get older. This quid pro quo mindset needs to disappear. The reason we should do good things for young people is because we are adults and they are children. It is a simple acceptance of responsibility. People should be kind and caring to the elderly, but again, not out of some sense of debt, but merely because it is the right thing to do. Ultimately, it is not so hard to be kind to children that we should expect some form of repayment at an unspecified date in the future.

The comment about our days at work making the world better, having no effect, or making it worse relates to how we make our money. A drug dealer or pimp makes the world worse every day that they wake up. That will be true until the day they wake up and decide to change their lifestyle. If they never make that choice, their negative impact continues until they die, and hopefully, they will have hurt the fewest number of people possible by the time that day arrives.

For other people, such as online ticket scalpers, they are more or less in a self serving mode. They offer no service to others, and they create no product. By buying up tickets, then reselling them for a higher price, they can feed themselves, and make a tidy profit, but if they all disappeared, we would just buy our tickets for the correct price, and they would not be missed. Carpenters, plumbers and farmers are the people who allow every other field of endeavor to exist. We must have food to eat, water to drink and shelter from the elements. Take those careers away, and no person would care about any other item. These are the people who serve as the foundation of our society.

Carpenters, plumbers and farmers are easy to respect, we see these people work hard, and we see the products of their labors. Education is different from many professions in that the end product reflects as much the choices and abilities of the students, as it does the effort of the collective group of teachers who touched that student's life. When a carpenter measures and cuts a piece of wood, the length and angle of that cut are 100% in the carpenter's hands. Success in education is advocated for by the teacher, but also controlled by the student. Success for a teacher will vary on a student by student basis. Sometimes success means helping a kid get into an Ivy League university, other times, it means giving the kid the will power to get to graduation and not drop out. That is the interesting thing for a teacher, the amount of effort exerted helping one kid graduate, might equal the effort exerted helping another student gain acceptance into an elite university. Each student is equally deserving of the teacher's attention. A teacher's goal should be to help each student achieve whatever their personal goal is.

The Kids

To convey the reality to a student that the student can change the trajectory of his or her life, and have that student believe it, is half of the battle in education. Teachers deal on a regular basis with questions from students like: "Why do I have to learn this? I will never use it." My answer to that is to explain that while I was working during high school as a fry chef, I never needed to know any significant facts. When the red light on the fryer lit up, the fries were done. Then I would take them out of the fryer and put salt on them. If that scenario basically covers all of the student's life goals through retirement, well, maybe they don't need to learn much. Otherwise, the information being presented in any class will, for someone, meet a prerequisite for future course work in preparation for entering a career field. Each subject's course work will vary in importance for an individual student based on career goals. Even within a particular course, each individual bit of information may not be applicable to a student's future success. This does not change the fact that the wider the knowledge base a person has, the more readily their mind can absorb additional information and make correlations with future pieces of input.

While the information presented at a high school level in any particular course will have a varying degree of value to each individual student, ignorance is never valuable. Each piece of information is definitely valuable to someone somewhere, and if it does not lead to financial rewards at a professional level, it may help in some area of personal life. Training after high school will refine a person's studies to specific trade related information; prior to that, education cuts a wide swath across all fields of human knowledge.

It is not always possible to successfully advocate obtaining knowledge for the sake of obtaining knowledge. At times it is important to mention that future college recruiters will be looking into a student's transcripts. The transcripts will convey a sense of the student's ability to complete assignments and learn material. Students should also know that their brain actually goes through physiological changes during the learning process, giving them a stronger mind, more capable of receiving and processing information. When axon terminal end bulbs produce neurotransmitters more efficiently, or myelin sheaths are formed around axons, the rate of nerve impulse transmission increases, building stronger minds. Building those stronger minds must be the goal of education, the goal must not merely be to funnel kids through a system.

There is perhaps a simple analogy here related to my high school job flipping burgers (over time, I moved up from the fryer). If you look at the cooks, cashiers and managers in a restaurant that serves unhealthy food, and you look at their counter parts in a restaurant which sells health food, you will see their procedures are identical. The customers pay similar prices, and the process of packaging and charging for the food is identical. The difference is in the nutritional value, and how much the recipient gains from the transaction. When focused on health, I would prefer a carrot, apple, spinach cocktail from Fruition over greasy fries. Likewise, in education, the procedures from teacher to teacher and school to school have striking similarities. The difference is in how much the students gain from their exposure to the process. It is the responsibility of teachers to insure that they are serving a "nutritional" education to the students. The procedural steps of: registering kids for classes, distributing report cards and having graduations are the same everywhere.

The essence of the teaching profession is not to merely come in, and go through the motions, but to transmit to the students the importance of their own education.

Some students have told me that they only do well in classes where they like the teacher, I will tell them that the teacher in question will receive the same paycheck regardless of whether the student does or does not pass the course, so: "Why spite yourself? Always do the best you can." It is hard to convince every student of certain truths, but it is important to convey truth to the child, and then hope they accept good advice.

The Professionals

Sometimes it is not the students who need to be convinced of what seems obvious, but the educational professionals. I recently attended a conference on Core Content Standards in science. After the presenter asked who still teaches kids about the 6 simple machines, most hands went up. He then condescendingly looked at us with a smirk and said: "Why? They are not in the standards.

Stop wasting time teaching things that we have decided are not important." In answering his question, I explained the importance of utilizing simple machines for scores of everyday tasks, their importance in designs generated by engineers, and explained how it is a great lesson for younger students who learn the basics of the machines, but that simple machines can later be studied in greater depth by older students who can also learn about mechanical advantage, and work and power generation, thus adding in several mathematical formulas which give a practical application to the use of math, while strengthening each student's mind. This greatly bothered him. His face reddened as he said: "Don't waste your time teaching them; they are not in the standards!" My next comment seemed to bother him: "The standards are not God." That caused his voice to ascend into a shriek; "Yes, they are God!" A lady, trying to defuse the conversation raised her hand and made this statement to the instructor: "So what you are saying is that as long as we follow your standards, our kids will become more competitive globally?" With a sigh of satisfaction and a smile of relief, he responded: "Yes." He then clicked to the next slide in his power point presentation, it read, in bold letters: OPEN MINDED DISCUSSIONS ARE ESSENTIAL TO FURTHERING OUR KNOWLEDGE OF SCIENCE.

Due to the unsuccessful nature of my exchange regarding simple machines, I was hesitant to continue participating, as there was no point in trying to convince the man doing the presentation that knowledge had value. Later, he presented an assertion that kids now-a-days only need to know how to find the information. In other words, a student who can type words into a Google search has completed his or her education. An educated person should know how to use a computer but should not depend on one for recall of basic facts. Intelligence is what a person knows when they are unplugged from technology.

Later, his associate made a mocking comment regarding how he had attended a science class where students were learning about mitosis. He assured us that he has done quite well in life with no knowledge of mitosis. If the people who direct the educational process are cavalier about the lack of importance in absorbing knowledge, to whom can we then turn for a greater commitment to erudition? Despite feeling guilty pointing out where he was wrong, it seemed irresponsible to allow these men to downplay so many forms of knowledge. In response to his minimizing the importance of learning mitosis, I mentioned the use of colchicine, which interferes with the production of spindle fibers during metaphase of mitosis and how this knowledge has allowed scientists to create polyploid strawberries which provide higher harvests. This did not send him over the edge, but he did let everyone know that such information should be reserved for graduate students.

A man responsible for directing teachers in how to educate students was deficient himself in understanding that unless high school students comprehend the basics, they will not become graduate students. Even in American universities, you are as likely to find a foreign student earning an advanced degree in math or science as you are an American student. On September 15th of 2005, William A. Wulf testified before the 109th Congress that over 50% of Ph.D.s in engineering are awarded to foreign students. A one to one, American to foreign student ratio, in American schools is an embarrassment. It means that a foreign student in a second language is more competitive in science and math that an American student in his or her first language.

The diversity found in American schools is good. We have foreign students, just as overseas schools have American students, but when our graduate students are staying away from math and science and leaning towards majors where fluff is given equal weight with cold hard facts, something is clearly amiss. We need to encourage students to build skills in math and science.

Teaching is a career which can lead to a periodic longing for a career change. Despite that, there remains the reality that as a teacher you can positively influence the life of a young person and without people willing to positively influence this next generation of young people's lives, America is winding down its time as a beacon of light, as we have far too many adults willing to influence this next generation towards negative behaviors. It is not for teachers alone to seek redirection for America, but rather every adult in our nation.

Regardless of what profession a person has chosen, we can all positively impact the next generation as we choose what we will embrace within our culture, and what we will disavow.

CHAPTER THREE
Cultural Influences

"America is great because she is good. If America ceases to be good, America will cease to be great."
~ Alexis de Tocqueville

Nature abhors a vacuum. In a culture, there are no vacuums. When parents and communities fail to provide proper nourishment for a child's soul and mind, a profit minded entity will fill that void. What is filling that void at this time in our country's history would have never been tolerated at any other time in our history. The horrible stories that fill our newspapers are the direct result of the manner in which this void has been filled. To diminish the value of human life, and to increase the amount of brutality in entertainment will increase the level of violence in a society. In that many of the negative forms of entertainment which have achieved popularity in recent times are forms of entertainment geared for boys, we should not be surprised that boys have been more negatively influenced than girls.

There are more positive influences available to our children than one might realize, we just need to pick them up, shine them up, and show them off. Still, it is essential to stem the flow of evil into our culture if we are to highlight the good.

There are many issues at this time which more readily affect boys than girls. There are gender inequalities in special education classes, gender inequalities in prison rates, gender inequalities in school dropout rates, etc. This is not to say that gender equality in rates of imprisonment would be a good thing. The absolute minimal rate of imprisonment would be the best thing. However, it is impossible to believe that high rates of incarceration are good for anyone. Certainly not the children whose father is unavailable to care for them, certainly not for the wife whose husband is absent. Certainly not for the active participants in society who must suffer lost income due to taxes which help maintain the prisons, and help care for the single mother households caused by these high incarceration rates.

Many people link the trouble with boys to the reality that when a parent leaves their family, it is most likely going to be the father. Thus the adult whom children are most likely to be cared for by, and concomitantly respect the most will be their mother. Children need to respect both parents; this is most easily done when both parents are respectable, but honoring your mother and father should be done regardless of circumstances. The notion of being respectful to one's parents appeals to a child's sense of duty. It then becomes the duty of the person being treated respectfully to understand their own need to be respectable. While every child has their own story, we need to accept the reality that schools cannot fix issues they were never design to fix. Should we then ignore behavioral problems with boys, or place higher expectations on them? Placing expectations on men is of greater value than offering carte blanche forgiveness for misbehavior, as if my gender is somehow understandably inferior. Boys can best learn to be men from men. American men need to weed through the myriad misrepresentations of what manhood is. It is neither professional wrestlers, nor shock jocks who represent what it is to be a man.

Despite a wide array of issues with which my gender is currently struggling, there is no wall separating men from women in society. When we read about abuses of women in the military, or abuses suffered by teenage girls at the hands of boys raised in this culture we must be willing to face head on that we are reading about our own failure to oppose what is wrong and champion what is right.

While men need to reassess the falsehoods we have accepted regarding manliness, women need to decide if they want to worship Lorena Bobbitt, while accepting the slide of men towards greater depravity, or do they want to more greatly appreciate and encourage the men in our culture who choose to be gentlemen. It is better to encourage people to act with compassion than to seek excuses to act viciously.

Having the belief that education is a vital link in preventing societal problems creates a more discerning analysis of how opportunities are distributed. If education is to be the springboard to success in society, access to the springboard must be as egalitarian as possible. It is great to see flyers announcing programs to strengthen student ability in science. I am saddened though when the flyers exclude boys. They never say: "boys are unwelcome here". They will say "Science fair for high school girls who are interested in careers in engineering".

We currently have a 60% to 40% gender inequality in college attendance favoring females. In that unskilled employment opportunities have dropped from 60% of the work force to less than 20% of the workforce over the past half century, we cannot be indifferent to either gender falling behind in academic achievement. This leads me to ask: Why are we excluding boys from opportunities open to females when the reverse would never be tolerated? Often my best students are female, achieving a level of success with no comparison in their male counter parts. I am very happy to see such success, but wish it was more equally achieved across gender lines. This is the reason I disagree with female only enrichment opportunities at lower levels. Other problems and challenges faced by our children cross all barriers. However, for at least this moment in history, boys are in need of help. Some universities now offer gender biased admittance, excusing boys from needing high grades and high SAT scores. Giving them easier access to university acceptance despite low ability, will only further water down our intellectual strength. Let's build up their abilities, rather than excuse inferiority. When opportunities for academic enrichment are presented, they should be offered equally to both genders.

When people talk about achieving parity for the sexes, statistics can be deceiving. A look at data from the Bureau of Labor Statistics shows that in 1979, women earned 62% of the income of their male counter parts. That improved to 82% by 2011. However, what those statistics do not show is the fact that in

1979, men were earning a little above $16 per hour, when women were earning a little over $10 per hour. By 2011, men were above $13 per hour, and women were above $11 per hour, meaning the salary gap dropped, because men's incomes dropped. That salary drop occurred during a time when inflation decreased the value of a 2011 dollar by 31% compared with the value of a 1979 dollar based on the amount of goods a dollar could purchase.

Another reason gender gaps in salaries can be deceiving is due to the dynamics of individual families. If a wife chooses to stay home and raise the children, her income will suffer, but that is an income loss for both a male and a female, as husband and wife share the burdens of raising a family, and they share the finances. If a husband stays home with the children, the situation still leaves a loss of income for the family. In that there is no price that can be put on a happy family, economic standards can not rate the success or failure of such a situation.

As an educator, any problem in society will eventually become a problem we teachers must contend with. The question then becomes: Should a problem in a school just be a problem that can be addressed because adults are in the building who should be mature enough to solve such problems, or should we create more levels of staffing? It does not matter if that problem is intellectual, social or emotional, the better the staff of a school is on a person by person basis, the fewer "specialists" we will need. We currently are focusing on bullying as a way to overburden taxpayers with more administrative experts.

Bullying is a problem that is universally recognized as a major concern throughout our schools. For teachers who chose the profession specifically due to a deep felt concern for young people, it is impossible to not be deeply affected by tales of student to student abuse. Growing up chubby, AKA fat, hefty, husky (well you get the idea), I was no stranger to bullies as a child. My last encounter with a bully that ended with me on the losing end occurred in 10th grade. A former friend had begun playing with steroids, and chose to give me a beating one morning. I did not want to fight, as we had been friends throughout middle school. Since that was a one way opinion, the conclusion of the fight was pretty well predetermined.

The day was instructional in a great many ways, which are helpful to me now in the classroom. One of the most important events of that day happened after the fight, when we all got on the bus. I sat in a seat, very dejected, and a classmate named Kevin came and sat next to me and said: "You OK?" A simple act of kindness means more than one can say on a day like that. Whenever a student is clearly having a lousy day, I will go out of my way to, in some way let my concern be known. If they later on come to me for more help and confide in me about what happened, I can do more at that time. If not, I know from experience that sometimes, a simple: "You OK?" can do wonders.

The event was also instructional in the sense that sometimes you must confront problems head on. Since then, when I am hit, I don't feel bad hitting back if turning the other cheek has already been tried.

Female bullies tend to function via character assassination and gossip mongering. In that this is the way in which dysfunctional teachers' unions function, teachers may not always be the best choice of people to address bullying. So who is left? Well the answer would be teachers who do not take part in the seedier conduct of union affairs. Teachers who have a strong conscience, and the backbone to do what is right when there is a great deal of pressure to do what is wrong. Students should be the ones, via votes to decide which adults in the school they want to have on the anti-bully committee. Students are the ones who know which adults are the most trustworthy; also the students lack the ulterior motives of trying to help teachers build up their resumes by padding them with titles.

Bullies need to be addressed unflinchingly and with an understanding that no human being on earth can more quickly become a pitiable "victim" in their own mind than a bully who has been stood up to.

During bully training it is taught that 85% of people are not involved in anything relating to the bully, or his or her victim, or his or her clique of toadies. 85% are merely indifferent bystanders, and their willing status to be mere bystanders is what empowers the bullies. An irony about those facts is that the training where I learned them was presented by a superintendent who was a bully, and he benefitted from the willingness of 85% of the staff to stand by indifferently as he chose teachers to bully and fire, thus opening up employment opportunities for friends of his.

In New Jersey, schools are now required to have anti-bullying specialists. The expense may be minimal, it may simply be that an administrator carries an additional title, or it could be that a teacher receives an extra free period to perform the duties, or some small stipend is awarded. Still, there is an expense attached.

While school yard fights are nothing new, the tactics employed by today's bullies are pure evil. The computer age has unleashed a shameless, faceless and unrelenting type of bully. For the victim, the abuse no longer ends when the school day ends. Today's unfortunate victims are hounded mercilessly 24 hours per day through online portals and social sites.

One case that deeply saddened me was reported by CNN.com on 10/7/10. A young girl seeking affirmation in a culture saturated by pornography decided to text a picture of her chest to a boy. Another girl accessed the photo, and then e-mailed it to others, who eventually had it spread all over the town. The ensuing string of verbal and physical attacks on the girl led her to commit suicide. The abuse did not end even after she killed herself by hanging herself in her bedroom. The online scorn persisted.

To mourn the girl is only part of this story. As a country, we also need to mourn the souls of the children whose vicious depravity was not even satiated by the girl's death. Young people like this girl are a reason to advocate for as much positive affirmation for children as possible. I have a fear of making children believe that every good deed comes with excessive praise, but a greater fear of having children think they need to degrade themselves to seek the approval of others. No child should ever wonder whether or not they have intrinsic value. No girl should ever feel that the gaining of a boy's attention should require her to devalue her own purity. However, as we increasingly sexualize younger and younger children, their lack of maturity when facing adult decisions will result in behaviors deleterious to the child. The tragedy of the conduct of the children in that case ties in to the fact that too many children are victims of adults in our society who knowingly prey upon their innocence.

Preying upon the innocence of youth is not limited to preying on small children. Older adults can also prey upon those emancipated young adults who do not yet know exactly where they will fit into society. In 2011 there was great interest in the case of a Rutgers freshman who, after being videotaped kissing a man, threw himself off of the George Washington Bridge. Appropriate scorn was cast upon the roommate who had invaded another's privacy by setting up a computer camera in the dorm to stream the encounter to another computer. However, the 30 year old man who had seduced the male college freshman was not portrayed in a negative light. Would any of you seek to protect or understand the lust of a 30 year old man who was cruising the freshman dorms looking for 18 year old girls?

Stories like this have become too common. There are stories about female athletes hazing younger girls by rubbing their faces in actual feces. Even that pales in comparison with the viciousness of Mepham High School's football team who raped younger teammates with golf balls, a broom handle and pinecones covered in burning liniment. Laura Williams of the Daily News wrote a follow up story on the case a year later, she published it on 8/13/04. Laura revealed that two of the four rapists received only probation, and only one of the four had been detained for longer than 6 months. As for the team members who merely enjoyed the show and cheered on their demented friends, they were back to football as usual. We have in many ways become an evil society; the lack of punishment shows a comfort with such evil. Are there times when a dad should handle justice himself? I am sure that had a parent of one of the victims taken justice in his own hands, the courts would have suddenly become capable of punishing a citizen.

In such a climate, a teacher's kindness should be an example of how to treat others. That kindness must not be a front for inept cowardice in the face of times that require firm discipline. Keep in mind that it is impossible for a teacher to get through a year teaching without having people mad at them at one time or another. A teacher's goal should be to have the people who were in the wrong mad and have the people who were in the right pleased. Ultimately, if the people who were in the wrong at a later time in some way acknowledge that they caused a problem, there have been two victories, the first being doing what was right on behalf of the victim, the second being the generating of some increased sense of responsibility in the bully.

One thing to ponder is this: How does an adolescent become a creature who would ram a pinecone into a smaller child's rectum? Many of today's issues are parenting issues. By means of explanation, whenever you hear about a horribly violent crime committed by a juvenile, you are very likely to also hear about the parents rushing to the child's defense. They will threaten lawsuits, they will abuse the victims to intimidate them from pressing charges, but they will not acknowledge that for 15 years, they failed to teach their children right from wrong. They failed to monitor and censor what their children had been exposed to, and they failed to model behaviors based on kindness and caring. Rape is not a step one deviation from correct behavior.

When considering what is out there in our culture and available to be absorbed from media such as television, the common advice is: If you don't like what is on the TV turn the channel. It makes sense, and it works for adults. However, when trying to understand what is going on culturally and what influences our children are being exposed to, "turn the channel" is bad advice. Adults should keep the channel where it is and see what children are very likely choosing to watch. Telling adults to turn the channel is kind of like being in a situation where you see drug deals going on in your neighborhood and you are told to just look away as the best means of responding.

When the stories that make our hearts ache for this country seem too common, we need to actively seek stories which will encourage us, and renew or faith in humanity. When the Mustangs of Macon Georgia provided an opportunity for an autistic boy to live his dreams of playing organized football, the result was a touchdown for that young man, and a sense of worth in the hearts of the young men of the Macon Mustangs, even more so their opponents, the NE Detroit Shamrocks that must surely have rivaled any positive feeling either team had even before or since enjoyed as a result of being an athlete. In each boy that day was displayed the most noble trait of humanity, the ability to care about another. The cost to the teams: one play.

When we see conflicting events associated with football, which are as far removed from each other as the North Pole is from the South Pole, we need to seek answers for why our culture has turned in such a direction. It is also important to encourage more of what is right in our culture. As far as the culture goes, a critical analysis of the changes in our culture needs historical context. Each independent change can then be linked to greater changes within our culture. Our founding fathers guaranteed freedom of speech so that people could seek a redress of grievances with their government free of the threat of retribution for opposing a decree issued by a monarch.

The concept of "free speech" has been so thoroughly twisted that the Supreme Court of the United States in June of 2011 sided with the makers of video games that allow the players to simulate situations where every imaginable form of brutality and vile degradation can be inflicted on characters in the game. The Supreme Court has permitted its sale to children. In the case, which pitted the State of California against the Entertainment Merchants Association, morality lost, and the children of our county lost. Of course, the makers of the game have to label that the game is for "mature" audiences. (The word "mature" needs to be returned to the context of being a person with strong values developed over time.) How can any educated and morally stable person make such an interpretation of free speech from the Constitution of the United States?

We are devastated when year after year we read stories of horribly violent atrocities occurring in schools. Sandy Hook Elementary School's nightmare was the most tragic event of 2012; such events must motivate us to: #1.) Refuse to allow the saturation of our culture with violence and #2.) Motivate us to replace the morally repugnant forms of entertainment with wholesome forms.

The price for our accepting an increasing level of base conduct in our society can be quantified. The freedom we have in America was never meant to be a form of anarchy, where everyone did as they pleased. Rather, it was meant to be a type of freedom where we choose the laws by which we live, rather than having laws imposed upon us by a monarch. As we move into the anarchy of thought and conduct that some advocate for, the quantifiable price is seen in many areas.

Is There a Dollar Value?

One quantifiable price of a country which has lost its moral compass is the cost of health care. In 2002, the Centers for Disease Control showed the price of mental health care at 300 billion dollars. This is not all related to the destruction of moral responsibility. Alzheimer's, Parkinson's, schizophrenia, etc. have always been condition we needed to content with out of love for our family members. What I ponder is: Are there unnecessary costs of mental health care created by our increasing comfort with questionable conduct?

Consider a story reported by Reuters on 11/11/11. A thirteen year old boy raped a five year old girl at a McDonalds in Ohio. That tragically scarred little girl will now need counseling and psychiatric help to deal with her trauma. The boy will receive psychiatric help and detention, all at a cost to the tax payers. We are left to question whether the boy is a deviant, criminal sociopath or other and how did he arrive at such a state. The price for this treatment is a quantifiable measure of the price for accepting evil within our society. The harm done to that little girl can never be quantified. We can only overcome such tragedies with an equally immeasurable outpouring of love.

Speculation as to what caused the boy to grow up in such a way is fruitless unless we choose to make the necessary changes to ensure that never again will a child grow up in such a way. Unfortunately, it can not be done, there will always be evil in society, we can only hope for better, and work to reduce the prevalence of such evil. Perhaps it was the boy's family, perhaps it was society that instilled such sexually charged violence into his psyche. Either way, people are employed in the psychiatric health field at a higher rate than would be necessary in a world where parents raised, loved and cared for their children properly.

In a school, each additional counselor will raise the budget in that district by $100,000. When we look at industry, certain occupations create a product which leads to increased revenue. Mental health care does not raise revenue via generation of a product, it returns people to a state where they can proceed with life at an appropriate level of efficiency. People in mental health care have chosen a noble profession, and an essential one. We as a culture need to make the changes which will minimize the number of patients created because they are the victims of the abuse of people tainted by new cultural norms. That little girl who went to a McDonalds should not need therapy; she should have never been harmed.

There are patients who have had a need for help created by tragic circumstances, misconduct of others, or parents who have abnegated their duty to their children. Those children in the last group are, due to their parents, forcing workers into mental health care when those workers could be employed in a job that stimulates the economy via production. Perhaps they could not be employed at all, but living in a world where diminished expenses allow one income households to pay the bills. If people could work fewer hours, the more likely it would be that children would have a parent at home to care for their emotional needs throughout their developmental years.

Brian Welch, whose fame sprang from his role as a musician in a heavy metal rock band had a conversion event upon hearing his own daughter singing words to one of his own songs. He did not want his own daughter to sing what his band sings. Within the context of seeing his daughter exposed to what he exposed other parents' children to, his whole world changed and he could no longer associate himself with his own music. That is compelling. However, we cannot wait for every musician or performer to have a revelation about their own product. As adults in a society, we should already be cognizant of what children are exposed to, and what effect it will have on them.

It is possible to create a smaller sphere of happiness within the greater realities of what is going on in our world. There are infinitely more happy moments in life than sad moments. Recently, while watching the Wizard of Oz with my daughters in a local theater which plays vintage films, my attention was focused more on my daughters and their friend than the movie. They would giggle, and squirm around with delight while watching the Lion's hijinks. They would mimic his movements, and laugh out loud at his facial expressions. My youngest needed a hug when the flying monkeys arrived, but otherwise, she loved every minute. We are not so far removed from a healthy culture that we need to lament too severely. We are far enough removed from a healthy culture that we dare not fall into indifference.

Think of our prison system. Millions of inmates who could be generating positive revenue for the Gross Domestic Product are instead draining the system by having their daily needs provided for by the taxpayers. Correctional officers work a very difficult and dangerous job. Again, we see men and women who work very hard. They work under trying circumstances, and yet the positive side of the GDP ledger is not improved by their efforts. This is not to say that many people go to work with the goal of improving the GDP. People work to support themselves and their families. It is the responsibility of government to achieve an economy where people are working in such a way as to improve the positive aspect of the nation's GDP.

There are times when even people who are "productive members" of society leave us with nothing to show for money spent and effort exerted. Take for example, a fictional, "Joe the tattoo artist". His customer wants a $300 tattoo reading "I love Maria forever and always" with a little heart under it. Joe does a beautiful job, and the customer is highly impressed with his ink. Two months later, (following the break up), the customer goes to Suzy the tattoo removal technician. The customer pays $300 to have the tattoo removed. After $600 being spent, time and effort being invested, there is nothing to show for it. That is of course a situation of personal choice, but we have a great many societal safety nets in place to help people survive through their bad choices, and I would rather pay less taxes, and make my own good choices, while paying for my own bad choices than to have someone who may be receiving public support spending hundreds of dollars on bad choices. These may seem like silly thoughts, but as our national debt passes 15, 16, 17 trillion dollars, I can't help but wonder: How are we spending this borrowed money? What do we have to show for it? The nation borrows it, it filters into our economy, and what do we have?

We will always live in a society where some people make good choices, others make bad choices. Issues arise in schools for the whole gamut of reasons. Teachers need to worry about a great many important issues. A child receiving free school lunch and having a parent covered in $2,000 worth of "body art" is not an issue of national or personal wealth, it is an issue of faulty priorities. At the same time, reduced lunch and free lunch programs are part of what we value in our national psyche, the notion that we will not let children suffer because of their parents' circumstances. To that end, an innovation in free lunches that deserves applause is the use of debit cards in lunch rooms. Some students have an account that their parents fill, other students have cards that the school fills, but there is no way of knowing who is getting reduced or free lunch. This eliminates social pressures which might inhibit children from using the program if they had to use tickets which were clearly associated with free lunches.

While some people in schools are dealing with severe abuses of children, most teachers have fortunately never had such an extreme crisis to handle. Handling smaller crises on a regular basis is a major key. Some things that are trivial can become gigantic when dealing with a parent who is emotionally unstable. Many times, teachers deal with minor issues which become big deals only because Americans are living in a society where getting one's own way has been elevated to an art form by some of our neighbors.

I've had situations where correcting a child leads to severe backlash from parents even though I make a point of correcting students as gently as possible. Teachers need to stand their ground in such situations. Those are the times when it is good that tenure exists. It is much better for a child to experience the minor inconvenience of slight discipline, than to grow up with a feeling that consequences do not exist. The U.S imprisons 715 people per 100,000 citizens. For most countries, it is closer to 100 people per 100,000 residents. If we would administer discipline in more effective ways to our youth, while still letting the child know that they are cared about, and not disliked, children might be less inclined to fight against discipline or feel belittled by it. Discipline should be presented as a means of clearing the slate. Whatever happened that was wrong needs to be addressed and then after discipline, forgotten.

Comparing minor situations to more severe situation, some parents will, when their child is punished, act as if they want a teacher to lose his job, so imagine the conduct exhibited by a parent with a child accused of rape when learning that their child is facing jail. These are the situations modern schools are trying to contend with. This is why tenure exists. I will not say it is never abused, but I will say that it does have its purpose. One change that should occur is for unions to exempt non-tenured teachers from paying union dues, as a non-tenured teacher will be let go at the drop of a hat with no reason needing to be given.

Sunny Side Up

Before I create too depressing of a picture, I should also mention that I am daily encouraged by the wonderful young people I am blessed to spend my days with. In a land of 300 million people, the kids who are wonderful in every way often get overlooked by news agencies, but their individual impact on fellow human beings is positive and rejuvenating. Every day I come home happy to have spent the day with the students I teach. They encourage me in too many ways to cover: kindness to me, to each other, completion of excellent work, etc. The world is full of great kids, and I am blessed to spend my days caring about them, and being around them. Newspapers may take an approach regarding stories that: "If it bleeds it leads". Therefore newspaper stories will have a disproportionate number of negative to positive stories. Always take time to acknowledge the positive things that happen in your own life, and on a daily basis, try to leave something positive in someone else's life. If reading the negative stories with which newspapers are saturated gets a bit too cumbersome, Google "happy news stories". There are (thankfully) certain websites which specialize in sharing good news.

The things it takes to be a great parent are not complicated. Working in a town, you get to know the families. You will see things that explain how parenting is done properly. I once had a student names Katie. One morning before school, I saw her and her father at the local diner. When I went to say hello, I asked how often they went to the diner for breakfast. Her father explained that every Friday, he would take one of his children to the diner, and on that Friday it was Katie's turn. Katie, I should mention was a wonderful young lady. Surely, such time together gave father and daughter an opportunity to talk and connect, which helps in raising a child. Just as surely, the feeling of being treated in a special way left an emotional, golden nugget in the girl's heart which is just as significant as the positive effect of talking to each other. Letting kids know they are loved is invaluable.

Caring about kids is one of the most important pillars of education. That needs to be a natural part of a person's make up if they are to truly excel in the field. Not everyone likes kids. W.C. Fields famously said that if he ever wanted to hear the pitter patter of little feet in his house, he would hire a midget as a butler. Other qualities of stand-out educators can be picked up in unexpected places. Serving in the United States Coast Guard, and being stationed on an icebreaker in the Arctic Ocean was an important experience for me.

So much of what I learned in the Coast Guard has helped me in teaching. What not to do as a leader was a good lesson to learn. Teachers are the leaders in their classrooms. When you are in a subordinate position, you want to follow orders because they are the right orders given by a person with good judgment. You do not want to follow bad orders just so the senior person can demonstrate their power. A teacher should want kids to follow directions because those children know that what the teacher is doing is in the students' best interests. Making good decisions exhibits responsible conduct. Making and getting away with bad choices shows power. Ours is a country founded on a belief that people trusted with power may abuse it; therefore each individual is entrusted to be responsible, rather than powerful. A system of checks and balances needs people who believe in appropriate conduct. Suppose a school's system of checks and balances is based on the give and take between the union and the administration, yet both the union president and the district superintendent are of questionable character: What can be done? If people are unwilling to stand up for what is right, nothing. People need to believe that they have the power to be vocal regarding their concerns while respecting the opinions of others. We certainly should not be a nation of sheep blindly accepting the decrees of our leaders. That is not our system of government or our system of leadership. We should expect that leaders can explain the purpose of their actions, and those actions should coincide with the advancement of the stated goal.

Caring greatly about what you are entrusted with should be foremost in a person's mind with any job, regardless of what they've been entrusted with. A teacher is entrusted with the psyches of young people. Anytime I feel I have made a bad judgment call, I will track down the student involved and clear up the misunderstanding. Having the ability to at least try and fix your mistakes is a blessing. It is easy for adults to forget what types of things were emotionally painful 30 years ago, while still young. I clearly remember two incidents when I joked around with a child in a way that would have made me laugh had I been on the receiving end of the joke, only to realize how much I offended the child. I felt horrible, and made sure to apologize to those children in front of the rest of my students. Balance can not be restored by apologizing in private for something that happened in public.

Trying to fix mistakes not only serves to rectify an error, but also implants more deeply in a person's own head the importance of avoiding the same mistake again. People with authority have the greatest ability to make mistakes with wide reaching impact. People with little authority have the least ability to cause big mistakes. Leaders need to be people with a long history of good decision making.

You do not know this, but via your tax dollars, you once paid for a 6 million dollar mistake. When our ship was in the Arctic, one of our helicopters went down due to failure of the tail rotor. Without a tail rotor, a helicopter cannot maintain lateral control, but altitude can still be controlled. Our pilot brought the helo down as gently as possible. The helicopter slid off of the ice flow onto a foot of the ice flow (a submerged ledge of ice attached to the flow). All crew members were fine, but the helicopter was submerged in salt water, destroying most of the high tech electronic equipment. The shell, however, was fine. We sailed the boat over, and attached the correct straps (for the given weight of the helicopter) to the helicopter and to the crane. We were then ready to hoist the helicopter. Here is where paying attention to the simple things pays off (or becomes costly). Water weighs eight pounds per gallon. This is the type of basic knowledge schools should dispense. Our submerged helicopter contained thousands of gallons of water. The straps which were the correct strength rating for the helicopter were not the correct rating for the helicopter AND tens of thousands of pounds of water. Still, a helicopter full of water was potentially not a problem. When giving directions to a crane operator, if you point your index finger skyward and circle rapidly, it means hoist rapidly. If you turn your palm upward, and slowly mince your thumb and fingers, it means lift slowly. The direction to lift slowly results in the water draining from the helo while it is lifted, and results in a helicopter being hoisted successfully, and then put back in action after the electronic equipment is replaced. The direction to lift rapidly while the helicopter is full of water results in the cables snapping and results in a helicopter imitating humpty dumpty on the Arctic Icecap. Well taxpayer, you paid six million dollars for humpty dumpty. I advanced farther on my trek to expect leaders to deserve, rather than demand respect. Teachers should deserve respect, not demand it.

Fixing education is just part of fixing our culture, but it is an important part. By providing more facts, and less opinion in education, we will build stronger minds. By demonstrating kindness rather than teaching it, we save time and money, and schools can focus more on transferring knowledge rather than character development. We must avoid tug of war curricula which address one problem while creating another. To say that reading anything is good, as it is still reading is wrong. If books are offensive and transmit questionable morals, we are creating problems we will later have to fix. America has many great people we can admire. We can learn history and morals at the same time. We can learn courage and determination from Tecumseh, we can learn compassion and devotion from Clara Barton, we can learn moral clarity from Billy Graham.

If students learn how to write a book report by reading a book which paints perversion, violence or irresponsibility in a positive light, we are going forward on one front, backwards on another.

The Grapes of Wrath will always be an object lesson in what true hardships really are. We are fortunate to have the vast wealth of our past to guide us. More than lamenting what is bad in our culture, we need to celebrate and embrace what is good in our culture and excise what is bad.

CHAPTER FOUR

Uneducated educators?

A child educated only at school is an uneducated child.

~ George Santayana

Are you educated because you have a degree? Does having a degree mean that someone jumped through prescribed hoops, or does that degree mean someone placed high demands on his or her cognitive development, and now have a head full of facts and the ability to employ them correctly? What does it mean to be educated, and how does the education teachers receive help them to educate students?

Any time two people are in disagreement the ceiling of comprehension is determined by the person of lesser intelligence. In education, many people believe themselves to be an expert because everyone in education is listened to when they speak. Listening to others is a blessing that teachers should welcome. When an orthopedic surgeon was kind enough to visit our school, it was a rare chance for me as a scientist to sit and listen to another person with great knowledge in a specialized area.

Teachers have knowledge of their discipline and it should be grown at every opportunity. Unfortunately, educators are also trained to implement curricula as directed. There is an element of critical analysis missing from this arrangement. If a person is implementing a curriculum whose content is unfamiliar to the instructor, the instructor must first make himself or herself an expert before presenting the material to the children. Days have limited hours, months have limited days. The question is: Will every instructor determine to become an expert in the content they teach? This is why it is critical that training in education be based more on the discipline the teacher will present rather than the pedagogy with which it is presented. Also, it should be understood that based on an area's socioeconomic makeup, strategies that work well in one area may not work particularly well in another area. Teachers need an intuitive ability to develop methods of presenting information in a way which is effective in the community where they teach. Basic facts of an academic discipline are the same regardless of where a teacher is employed.

If a teacher can attend a training seminar on how to present information effectively at a cost of $175 to the school district, they are considered educated in that technique. If the teacher can sit down with a child, and by questioning that child on what they do and do not understand, come to an understanding of how to better present the information to the child, the teacher is better educated and the student had their questions answered and the school district saved $175. Both teachers received an education in how to present information to a child. Only in example two did it directly help a child. So what does it mean to be educated?

R. Clarke Fowler wrote an article *The Heralded Rise and Neglected Fall of the Massachusetts Signing Bonus* in 2008. In the article, he mentions the "flunk heard round the world". When a teacher recruiting program offered bonuses to college graduates who were going into education, they first had to pass a test. 59% of the aspiring teachers failed that test. While that event was chronicled because it was tied to a major recruitment effort, there are low quality teachers who get through the cracks in the system and end up in classrooms. On a personal basis, I have seen teachers so deficient in knowledge of their subject that they compensate by wasting periods chatting with students and giving them "real world advice". I dismiss the advice both because it is bad and because I understand the source, but for kids the source is a teacher and kids are taught to respect teachers. Anecdotally, I have spoken with a superintendent who, while interviewing a candidate for a math position, asked the candidate to explain an eighth grade math problem to him as if he were a student. The candidate could not decipher the problem; his college transcript included two grades of A in college level calculus courses.

The 59% failures in the first example were educated people, the math teacher in the second example was an educated mathematician.

All teachers are considered to be educated, and yet some teachers regularly do very dumb things. Before I distance myself from the clan of teachers capable of doing very dumb things, I'll share that we all seem to do dumb things on occasion. While grading a chemistry test a number of years ago, it seemed that many students forgot to label the subatomic particles in the nucleus as protons of neutrons. Only after writing the same note on several papers did it occur to me that it would be better to fully write out: "Are these protons or neutrons", rather than what I was writing, which was: "P or N?" That looked very bad on paper.

Realizing your own mistakes is a good way to get an education. Too often, "getting an education" is associated with spending money on tuition and getting a degree at the end. Being educated is much more than that. If it were not, Father Guido Sarducci's Five Minute University would draw a very high enrollment.

Franklin

Ben Franklin was very proud of opening Philadelphia's first library. Actually, it was just a collection of books he and his friends were willing to share. As libraries took hold in the colonies, Franklin was proud and boasted that common American men were the intellectual equals of more highly born European men, and this thirst for knowledge was influential in making the colonists the type of men who would seek and gain freedom, and then found a successful form of government. He felt libraries had caused this distinction. The first book Ben Franklin read was John Bunyon's "Pilgrim's Promise". It is interesting that Franklin's first experience reading was with a book that is still in print today. Franklin believed in the invaluable nature of libraries and in the development of intellectual prowess among citizens of a republic. Here is his quote on the topic:

"Our people having no publick [sic] amusements to divert their attentions from study, became better acquainted with books, and in a few years were observed by strangers to be better instructed and more intelligent than people of the same rank generally are in other countries."

We should return to being a nation with fewer "publick" amusements. Our children grow up in a world where they never have a moment to be bored. Let them be bored sometimes. When they are bored, they will then explore their own imaginations. Boredom can be a friend of intellectual curiosity. Maria Montessori advocated never redirecting a child from a task they were enjoying and focused on. That is great advice. Let them stay focused. Let them develop an attention span through their own curiosity. Our mind is our greatest machine. Instead of seeking to develop it, we look to endlessly occupy it: music, videos, computer games, etc. A child left to their own devices may stay for 10 minutes or more just staring at the activities of an ant mound. Television provides endless flashes of light, and constantly changing stimuli. Does TV cater to our short attention spans or create them? Are there ways to diminish the symptoms and prevalence of ADHD that do not require drugs?

Ben Franklin's intellect is an excellent example of what can be achieved with the exposure to information he enjoyed as a printer. Likewise, Michael Faraday during his apprenticeship as a book binder and Albert Einstein during his time at the Swiss Patent Office developed superb intellects by absorbing the information to which they had access. We should have a greater appreciation of time when we can just sit, read and learn.

Lincoln

The following is from Doris Kearns Goodwin's book about Abraham Lincoln; (Team of Rivals, page 51). It illuminates how a boy who lived in a log cabin and who often had to walk as far as 16 miles away just to borrow a book became the intellectual equal of men from his generation who had access to the best universities of their day and libraries of vast resources.

Books became his academy, his college. The printed word united his mind with the great minds of generations past. Relatives and neighbors recalled that he scoured the countryside for books and read every volume "he could lay his hands on". At a time when ownership of books remained "a luxury for those Americans living outside the purview of the middle class," gaining access to reading material proved difficult. When Lincoln obtained copies of the King James Bible, John Bunyon's Pilgrim's Progress, Aesop's Fables, and William Scott's Lessons in Elocution, he could not contain his excitement. Holding Pilgrim's Progress in his hands, "his eyes sparkled, and that day he could not eat, and that night, he could not sleep."

When printing was first invented, Lincoln would later write, "the great mass of men ... were utterly unconscious, that their conditions, or their minds were capable of improvement." To liberate "the mind from this false and underestimate of itself, is the great task which printing came into this world to perform."

Hidden Blessings

Any chance to lose oneself in quality books is a blessing, even if it is a blessing in disguise. Sometimes a love of reading becomes manifest in unexpected places.

During my time in the Arctic, I was upset with the Coast Guard. My recruiter had mislead me about an upcoming Officer Candidate Class, so I was washing dishes on a ship, having just spent 6 years doing menial labor to pay for college. The OCS class I was told I could enter in 6 months was actually 18 months away. I had the typical angst of a guy with a girl back home. There is a World War II song with the lyrics: "Don't sit under the apple tree with anyone else but me, till I come marching home". Times have changed regarding what a service man overseas worries about. In boot camp, the yeoman who signed everyone up for the G.I. Bill had told me that since I already had a bachelor's degree I was ineligible, I later learned, he was wrong, but having already declined the bill, it was lost. Seeking a way to pay for my master's degree was one of the reasons I had joined. Piece by piece, everything I had joined for was falling apart. I wanted to work on environmental issues, (the CG response to the Exxon Valdez spill was what caused me to commit to the service) instead, when our propeller was damaged, we were forced to pump oil contaminated bilge water into the pristine Arctic Ocean.

Despite the reality of a rare opportunity, I was still too upset at numerous circumstances to really appreciate what I had, and so, the only solace I had was books. Reading incessantly was good. I took and passed all the tests I needed to cover me for two promotions. That amount of testing normally takes 2 years. After completing it in six months, our Chief Boatswain Mate chose to wait for me to show more esprit de corps while washing dishes before he approved my promotions. Learning to be excited about dishwashing as a college graduate did not happen, but eventually we got a new BMC. I was upset over temporary problems, however, what was happening was that my mind was changing. I had earned very average SAT scores coming out of high school. I struggled in college and I graduated college with a C+ average. I still was no scholar, but I was reading constantly. After all of that reading, I was on my way to earning the GRE scores which would qualify me for Mensa, and I was developing the study skills that would allow me to complete my master's degree in biology with a 4.0 GPA.

That change in my abilities is a major motivator for me as an educator. I do believe that students who struggle can overcome a slow start in academics. They must want to overcome deficiencies, but it is possible. The trend to free students from the responsibility to overcome the challenges that cause them to struggle is a harmful practice in many schools. Only when it is impossible for a student to overcome an obstacle should that obstacle be removed. If the obstacle can be overcome with effort and guidance, the student should exert the effort, and the teacher should provide the guidance.

The 20/20 vision of hindsight shows my lamenting those two years was a waste of time. If I could go back in time, I would have appreciated the great friends I had on that ship, enjoyed my opportunity to travel, and let everything else roll off my back. Difficult times often lead to positive redirections in life; looking towards the horizon during such times is an important part of getting through such times.

It was actually a great blessing to have been cutoff from all of the daily distractions of day to day life in the United States. There was no worrying about pennant races, social plans, or fashion statements at the Oscars. Contact with family and friends came through writing letters. The intellectual spark I had not experienced during my schooling was going full blast, and it was not being fully appreciated. It is impossible to look at those teachers who merely keep children occupied for 6 hours per day with busy work, and not lament the tragic waste of time. That time was given to teachers to train their students' minds in how to absorb and process information. Instead, often, mindless activities are taking place.

Heritage

Our founding fathers grew up in a nation where public schools did not exist, but education did.

Ben Franklin's legacy to this nation obviously goes far beyond introducing libraries to us, but we should never let the significance of that contribution fade away.

Our founding fathers were great thinkers. That does not mean they were always right, but it does mean that being in disagreement with them should only come after deep thought and consideration. In their time, a person could not jump through hoops to get the qualifications for a position; then, based on possession of a certificate work in a field where performance was subpar. Instead, reading, thinking and learning strengthened one's mind. Then with that strength of mind, a person would move into a position of authority. Of course, nepotism existed then, as it does now; however, there are very clear examples from that time period of people lifting themselves up by the strength of their wits.

Looking at Washington's great officers, we do not see people who trained to be military officers, but rather people whose intellects distinguished them. When they were called upon to serve in the military, they did so with aplomb. Henry Knox was a book seller, Alexander Hamilton a college student, Benedict Arnold an apothecary, Nathaniel Greene was a pacifist Quaker. There are more examples of course, John Glover the fisherman/soldier and others, but these illustrations will do. These were men, who, if called upon to present their "soldier's certificate" before being commissioned would have all been disqualified from service. Instead, they lived in a time when distinguished service, intelligence and character were of greater value than credentials. It is the nature of rebellion to do away with the old power structure and replace it with a more effective one. Perhaps this explains the controversy surrounding charter schools.

We need to look at our own ignorance with the understanding that in grades K-12, at a rate of $12,000/year/child, $156,000 will be spent on educating our children's minds. Why are any of those minds empty of facts? How can we ensure that future expenditures of $156,000 will lead to the intended results? Current remediation rates and drop out rates indicate that the intended results are not being achieved. The desired results are the creation of an educated and knowledgeable citizenry. How many times have you been told by a person that they were an honors students in a foreign language, yet cannot utter one phrase in that language? This statement is not made to criticize the student. They know no better. For schools to function well, the teachers must desiderate the intellectual development of the students. Judith Scott Clayton reported in her 2012 paper, *Improving the Targeting of Treatment: Evidence from College Remediation*, that we spend 7 billion dollars annually as a nation to remediate college students who are underprepared for college. Why are we paying twice for students to be minimally proficient?

While "school choice" is an important topic in the discourse regarding how to improve the schools our children attend, a simpler solution may be "teacher choice", where students sign up for particular teachers based on that teacher's reputation for efficacy. Teachers can qualify for a base salary and benefits due to employment in the district, with additional salary based on number of students. As things currently stand, should a teacher have 50 students, they will receive the same salary as a teacher with 120 students. Moreover, teachers who distribute little knowledge receive the same salary as teachers who prepare students for future success.

Knowing what is really going on in a school is an area where boards of education may present themselves as a weak link. Some teachers know how to "work the board". A board member cannot work at their own full-time job, and truly know what is going on in the school on a day to day basis. The most manipulative teachers will see to it that their views are heard on a regular basis by open eared board members. An actual educator is busy with the industry of educating children, and lacks the time to play games. Outside of those manipulative teachers, most information board members receive will be from the administrators whose six figure jobs depend on the opinions of board members. A teacher who presents truth to a board of education which is in contrast to a tale told by an administrator is risking his or her job.

The teacher choice scenario is imperfect. Some special needs students need one on one attention for the entire day, hence certain teachers will be in a different category. In very small schools, there may only be one teacher who works in a particular discipline, so students who have to take that course will have no choice in the instructor. In other areas, it could ease the decision process of administrators. If teacher X has 50 students signing up for a particular course, while another teacher offering that same course has only 10 students registered, it makes it easier for the administrator to assign an instructor to the course.

I confess to some prejudices against education as an industry. Perhaps you already picked up on that. These perspectives are based on taking science courses in college and only enough education courses to receive my teaching certificate. These courses were part of my certification program. The courses were unimpressive. They typically assigned a quotation regarding a common sense observation to an individual. For example: You and I both know that you can not understand a complex concept until you first understand the underlying basic concepts. Comprehension happens in steps, and a person needs to take that path step by step, eventually being able to apply what was learned and utilize the skills learned in ways which exceed what was taught. Well, if you can say that in as verbose a manner as possible, you have Bloom's taxonomy. Educators go on and on about Bloom's taxonomy. Of course, that is meaningless unless they have a great wealth of knowledge relating to the discipline they teach. If I have a high school senior, or even a college freshman who does not know how gel electrophoresis helps separate strands of DNA associated with specific genes from a chromosome, I can go back and again explain the biochemical structure of DNA, and how a restriction enzyme works, and then advance from that point. Bloom's taxonomy is helpful, but only if a teacher possess the perspicacity to identify the point of disconnect, and the fact base to retrace his or her steps and advance from the point of confusion. Moreover, once a student has passed into the synthesis phase of comprehension, a teacher must be sufficiently competent in the topic to discern the validity of the student's statements.

Educators should focus 99.9% of their effort on knowing their subject matter and trust common sense to guide them through the rest. If a teacher seeks to find where a student's knowledge lapses, then takes them from that place to the place where they need to be in order to succeed in class, they have applied Bloom's Taxonomy. The secret is not having memorized a sequence of steps as outlined by Bloom's Taxonomy. The secret is in taking the time to understand a child's questions and having a sufficient knowledge of the subject to bring the child's level of comprehension from point A to point B.

During one graduate level education class, a fellow teacher made an amusing quip. The class was taught in Jersey City, New Jersey, which has some rough areas. The teachers all came from North East New Jersey, including places like Newark and Paterson. As you may or may not know, Newark is a tough place to grow up. It is also a place with some wonderful kids. We were watching a Lee Canter video. Lee Canter has a very logical belief central to any effective philosophy on teaching: Disruptive kids ruin the educational experience of others and need to have their behavior addressed. That does not mean that all of his tactics will work in every environment. In one segment, he showed how by dropping marbles into a bucket whenever something good happened teachers were giving the kids an auditory and visual reminder that when the bucket is filled there will be a class reward. He then showed how by writing a student's name on the black board for class room offenses, then adding check marks for subsequent misbehaviors, teachers were giving students a chance to correct their behavior before getting the final check mark for a punishment. At that point, a lady named Elaine blurted out: "Now Johnny, the next time you stab someone, I will have to add a check mark next to your name."

This makes for an amusing story, but it does illustrate how earning an advanced degree in education includes lessons on how to drop marbles into a bucket. If a person studied the proper way to put marbles in a jar to modify behavior, but has never read the Federalist Papers, Grey's Anatomy, Shakespeare, etc. I would consider them an "uneducated educator". They know trite tricks of the trade, but lack in depth knowledge about a specific subject. Unless a curriculum taxes one's mind, forcing the physiological changes that lead to greater cognitive abilities, the class was not fully worthwhile. In taking a science class and learning how the use of dideoxynucleic acids has revolutionized the way DNA sequencing can be done at a significantly faster rate than can be done using gel electrophoresis and restriction enzymes, while knowing that someone else may have focused on marbles as a means of modifying student behavior it becomes clear that there is a disparity in what teachers bring to the table. Unions insure that there is no disparity in salary to reflect those differences. This diminishes the motivation for the most highly qualified people to remain in education.

It is the strength of a teacher's knowledge base that gives them the final say in why students should behave. Students should behave because the teacher has knowledge they want to share. When students absorb that knowledge, they will be more marketable in the work force and better able to care for themselves and their future family, if they intend on having a family. A teacher's authority lies in the goodness of their mission. Of course, having high school students makes it easier to convey that notion to the intended audience than it would be to convey the notion to elementary students. However, if the elementary school teacher truly believes in the goodness of their mission, and lives that belief, the students will not need to be told why their education is so important. They will just accept kind and good instruction.

I have had students who were known to be terrible behavior problems, students who other teachers gossip about in the teachers' room, hoping to have them develop reputations which lead to more frequent disciplinary write ups. That is an unadvisable approach to classroom management. Just talk to the kid. Earnestly explain to them the importance of a smooth running classroom, and they will more often respond positively. A teacher should just tell them straight up that a teacher's goal is to help a child succeed in life, and education is essential. If it does not work initially, a teacher should pursue the disciplinary course that is appropriate, but keep coming back to earnest discourse. Should earnest discourse and the occasional disciplinary intervention fail to turn a child around, major discipline becomes necessary. However, somewhere in the back of that student's mind will sit both the words they received and the time a teacher spent with them sharing those words of wisdom.

When behavior has been addressed, learning can occur.

The standardized testing we perform to assess whether or not children actually are learning, was discussed by Stephanie Banchero in the May 16th, 2012 edition of The Wall Street Journal. As is true with many articles, on divisive topics, the conclusion of pro or con was left open for the interpretation of the reader. In reading articles of that nature one should look to distill as many hard core facts from the reading as he or she possibly can. In that particular article, the number $4.35 billion stood out as noteworthy. That is a lot of money being spent on President Obama's "Race to the Top Initiative". It has been layered on top of President Bush's "No Child Left Behind Initiative". In other words, one level of bureaucracy has been padded with another level of bureaucracy. To date, the efficacy of the initiative cannot be quantified. The expense can be quantified.

Think of three carpenters, each with a shop in your town. Each has a wood shop in which you can see the work they produce. When you choose your carpenter, you pay him for his time, and the materials he needed to create your contracted piece, let's say a table and chairs. If you do not like the table and chairs he created, you would not go to him again, and you would not recommend him to your friends. We will call the arrangement "Carpenter Choice". School choice is a less expensive way to deal with the issues that one layer of bureaucracy on top of another have not succeeded in dealing with regarding our problems in education. Consider those three carpenters, if on top of paying for the carpenter's salary and the wood and nails to make your piece, you were also paying to have union oversight, an administration running their shop, an outside test source checking their competence, and legal fees to cover any mistakes they made, your table and chairs would become unaffordable. There would be too many piggies at the trough. Education is becoming unaffordable and it does not have to be that way.

The notion of "teacher choice" is just a version of school choice without the added need of sending kids on long bus rides to a distant school. In a 2012 article on teacher rating systems by Heather C. Hill et. al, evidence was quoted showing that 34% of variance in student achievement is tied to who their teacher was, and there is a ten percentile point connection on standardized tests for students based on who their teacher was. If schools have great teachers available, schools should let as many students as possible benefit from that resource.

A well educated educator is more than enough to educate a child. What is important is that children have access to one.

CHAPTER FIVE

Science and Society

Innocence about Science is the worst crime today.
~ Sir Charles Percy Snow

My opinion my not be yours: Science is the first and foremost of subjects a person should learn. Everything else is derived from science and should follow in importance. Then again, I enjoy fried bologna sandwiches, so my opinions are far from unassailable, and the advocates for the preeminence of other subjects have their own rationale.

Just Opinions

To study political science is to study rules made by people, adjusted by people and implemented by people. They may change with the times, they are different from nation to nation and era to era. To study political science is to study these words: "We hold these truths to be self-evident, that all men are created equal, that they are endowed by their Creator with certain unalienable Rights, that among these are Life, Liberty and the pursuit of Happiness". Studying political science also includes studying the thoughts of Mao, Stalin and Pol Pot, and seeing how despite the inherent evil in their conduct, each was effective in controlling a population of people. If politics is about control, they were champions. Political scientists also help us to understand what makes healthy cultures healthy. Science is different, it remains true and constant from culture to culture.

English literature is the studying of the ideas, convictions and experiences of the author. So, in the world of the humanities, we are studying the thoughts of another. Those thoughts are framed by the period of history when they were formed and they are influenced by the circumstances of the author. Literature can touch our hearts, bring important issues to light, but it can be a subjective art form, while science is always objective. Literature conveys deep emotional messages, puts history in perspective and broadens our horizons, but one event may be seen in a dozen different ways by a dozen different authors. Scientific facts remain constant regardless of who observes them.

The fine arts brighten our world, increasing the pleasure with which we live our day to day lives. Art at its best increases the beauty of this world, but forms of it can also normalize behaviors which are deleterious to a nation. Good or bad, it is a very important component of our world. When the renaissance occurred, the rebirth of art went hand in hand with the rebirth of rational and complex scientific thoughts. A well tuned mind appreciates the efforts of artists, and artists who generate great works understand their ability to add meaning and beauty to the lives of the rest of humanity. It is interesting how in areas where museums are rare, street art is not. The gift of a mural by someone like Banksy can become part of the community's fabric of identity, as was the case with his work on the Packard Plant. Banksy is a graffiti artist whose work recently became part of a dispute regarding its ownership. When people in a community feel a work of graffiti art is a gift for their community, it highlights the feeling that art is itself a gift for humanity. Scientific advancements give us the free time to enjoy the world of art.

History teaches us the important events which shaped our world and gives us people of historical significance from whom we may find inspiration. Science is one of the premier influences in history. Without science, the Wright Brothers do not fly, boats do not navigate, and astronauts do not land on the moon.

Math identifies the recurring nature of our world and therefore holds the hand of science. It extracts hidden patterns of repetition, and allows the prediction of future events based on mathematical certainties. It is better to calculate the tensile strength of a steel cable before building a bridge than to, go with the trial and error method of investing 100 million dollars, and then having some cars drive over the bridge to test if it will or will not collapse.

The study of foreign languages allows us to communicate with people throughout the world. While it is great to be able to travel and communicate, or to welcome foreign visitors while they visit us, we should have a national language. Teddy Roosevelt warned us about the inefficacy of a nation where communication occurs as if it were a conversation at the dining room table of a "polyglot boarding house". English should be our national language; however, after 6 years of Spanish, a citizen of the United States should be able to converse with a guest from Costa Rica. If you have ever heard the expression: "If people want to come to our country, they should learn English." You were probably listening to a person who, when travelling abroad, speaks English very slowly and loudly to their host. Yes, we should have a national language, and yes we should learn to speak one or two additional languages and no, it is not unpatriotic to post some signs in English and also another language. While English is the language of business, both Chinese and Spanish have more native speakers throughout the world. A well educated citizen should be bilingual. Every American needs to improve their ability in a foreign language; however, application of language skills will not come into practice everyday for everyone, but application of scientific principles is a daily task, even if it is just knowing that higher speeds decrease fuel efficiency in a car, or understanding how our diets influence our health.

Every subject should be a joy to learn about, but science remains in my opinion the keystone subject. Opinions of those who disagree should be considered suspect, particularly if they lack the sophistication and refined palate to enjoy fried bologna.

Realities

Without science, we would be so busy just trying to stay fed, as seven billion people on earth are not fed by gathering wild berries, and we would be busy burying the ceaseless stream of corpses due to diseases we did not defeat, that it is unlikely we would have quite so much time to enjoy all those other subjects.

Believing that science is the most important subject for people to learn and understand does not negate the great value in all other disciplines. It does not diminish the fact that my favorite type of recreational reading is historical and it does not take away from my great love of literature and the arts. However, the study of science also embodies the struggles of the people who made the advances that allow our population to thrive. Our population thrives although it is currently over 100 fold greater than the world population once estimated to destroy mankind. That we can feed such a population and provide them with clean water testifies to the great achievements in science. It should hopefully also alert us to the need to continue pursuing scientific advances. The mere act of drinking water will, in the future, be a testament to our ability to control water pollution and hydrate crops as efficiently as possible.

Science intertwines with every other discipline. We are greatly disadvantaged to have scores of politicians in Washington with limited knowledge of how the natural world operates. At times, we are blessed by persons of vision. Teddy Roosevelt was a visionary to create the National Parks System. The conservation and preservation of our natural resources, which some would argue has been insufficiently addressed, has at least been acknowledged in such a system, and therefore its maintenance has always remained within our grasp.

While discussing a general commitment to fluency in science as a means of understanding current events, there are specific examples we can look at. Currently, transgenic organisms and genetically modified organisms are increasingly important. There are situations where such creations are stored in labs, and their products are distributed in a controlled manner. Bacteria can be synthesized which produce human hormones by incorporating a gene for human traits within the bacterial DNA. That product is then distributed according to the protocols of the FDA.

Genetically modified crops pose different concerns. The possibility of cross pollination with local organic crops concerns some farmers. An inability to reproduce properly beyond one generation is a big concern for GMO crops, as sustainability of a food crop should not depend on perpetual distribution by a corporate entity. Putting terminator genes in seeds means they will not reproduce after one generation, meaning people cannot save seeds for the next growing season. Year after year, farmers must return to the corporation and buy seeds. Compare that mindset with the mindset of the scientists who died during World War Two rather than eat the seeds of the Pavlovsk seed bank during the siege of Leningrad. Seeds represent future crops, representing the feeding of humanity. Not everyone needs to be able to understand such topics on a par with the scientists who work in such fields, but in that our politicians regularly make laws concerning the implementation of scientific protocols regarding how we utilize such knowledge, it would be good if they could intelligently discuss such issues.

We currently need someone to emphasize the value of locally grown crops. Each state should have areas where development is denied, thus maintaining arable lands and diminishing our dependence on foreign crops, such as we regularly import from South American countries. We would also be minimizing the investment of fossil fuels as a means of delivering food to local communities via ships, then trucks. China has been a leader in developing apartment top green houses as a means of both beautifying urban environments while providing necessary crops. American political values are often held in contrast to China's communist government, however, we should isolate individual achievements in science, and separate them from association with conflicting political views when we look at what should be implemented in America. Many people speak about a concern for the deforestation of the Amazonian rain forest. It is idle talk without seeking to remove the motivation to clear cut the forests. Since forests are clear cut to plant crops for export, experimenting with urban agriculture would diminish the rate of deforestation by diminishing the need for creating more farmland.

Science as History

Loving history makes the lives of people like Tycho Brahe, Johannes Keppler, George Washington Carver, Louis Pasteur and to be honest, just about any scientist of note, fascinating. Their biographies make for consuming reading. It also puts in perspective the historical advances despite technological limitations of different eras. France could not have economically rebounded from the Franco-Prussian War without the help of Pasteur's advances in wine production and sheep farming. As a teacher, making the study of rabies, pasteurization and anthrax interesting can be a chore, but adding in little tid-bits about how Pasteur addressed such obstacles in historical context helps.

Telling students that the word vaccine is derived from the Spanish word vacca for cow, ties in nicely with the lessons of students who are studying Spanish. It still does not make learning about inoculations very exciting. Adding in details about how Edward Jenner vaccinated people against small pox by dragging a string through the draining puss of a cow pox patient, then making an incision in the skin of a healthy patient before dragging the puss covered string through that healthy patient's incision, makes young people much more comfortable with our current system of vaccination, and makes the story a little more interesting. Most children would prefer a doctor giving them a shot, rather than hearing: Hey Timmy, May I slice open your skin and drag some puss from Mary's sore through your cut?

Here is a tragedy for you: Ask a teenager to identify as many people as they can from this list: Snooki, Eminem, Charles Richard Drew, Lady Gaga, Robert Oppenheimer and Alexander Fleming. You know who they will identify. The tragedy lies in the fact that three of those people, are among the reasons the United States won World War Two. Alexander Fleming invented penicillin which had entered mass production by the 1940s, allowing soldiers to recover from injuries sustained on the battle field. Charles Richard Drew invented a method to allow blood for transfusions to last for extended periods of time, and of course, Robert Oppenheimer invented the atomic bomb. World War Two has been, to date, our pinnacle as a nation. Something happened since then, but it can be said with certainty that science, along with courage, and conviction allowed us to be victorious in a brutal conflict. Science should be used for peaceful purposes, but it also allows for strength in times of conflict, and that is good.

Conversely, when endless developments of new and better weapons take place during times that should be times of peace, we must remember Dwight Eisenhower's warnings about the military industrial complex. If our soldiers are being killed by weapons created in the United States and sold over seas, our greed has caused our demise. Beating plow shares into swords during war, and back into plowshares during peace time should be our goal. Our goal should not be to perpetuate the business of war. We need a season for plowshares. Protesting war is a political tool as much as a deeply held belief system. The myriad war protestors who insisted on expressing their view of war when George W. Bush was president, have ceased complaining about war since their candidate became the president who keeps troops overseas. Our two party system creates factions within a society where some people are not unhappy with poor leadership provided it is coming from the candidate they voted for. If a two party system was a good thing, George Washington would not have warned us about political parties. Association with like minded people increases likelihood of political success in pushing for certain changes; however, were associations weaker and of a shorter duration, people could affiliate on certain issues, without feeling obligated to continue that affiliation on other issues. Commitment to planks, rather than platforms would be liberating for politicians.

Prior to 9/11/2001, we held 5 trillion dollars in debt as a nation. That has tripled under two men; George Bush, who saw a need for military conflict and Barack Obama who promised to end the war within six months of taking office have both depleted our finances by engaging in war. Our love of war is devastating. 9/11 required military intervention, but we should be asking ourselves at this time: Does the loss of life for 8,000+ American soldiers coupled with the loss of hundreds of thousands of lives of people in the Middle East Expunge the loss of those 3,000 lives on 9/11? Why are we still engaged in an undeclared war?

My children are bilingual. In Japanese, "moto" means "more". "Arigatou" means "thank you". Whether with ice cream, presents, playing games or buying toys, I tell them: "know when to say Arigatou and not moto". In other words, if a person always wants more, and never stops to say thank you, that's enough, they will never realize how much they already have. I now want to give that same message to the president. It seems every time we capture or kill an Al Qaeda operative or Taliban officer we are told "Moto". More killing, more war. This must stop. We must return to a peace time economy, we must return to the application of science not as a way to better maim or kill our enemies but as a way to better feed cloth and shelter our citizens.

Drones neither know nor care the age or sex of their victims. In World War II, American soldiers took target practice on bull's eyes. In Vietnam, the military switched over to human silhouettes. The change diminished a soldier's hesitation when killing a human being. What made America greater than other nations was our belief in the value of human life. Each drone strike needs to be understood to be more than a hit on a video game, it is a loss of human life.

Science affects society for good and bad.

As a democratic republic, we need informed and intelligent citizens. Scientific thought is based on reason and an objective review of the facts. A scientific mind analyzing the cost of a decade of war and all of the societal changes it has produced will react differently than a mind trained to watch the news and regurgitate opinions the newscasters have read from their teleprompters.

One problem is that scientific thought and careful consideration of facts is difficult to sell to a society infatuated with glamorous celebrities. We need thoughtful people to provide such information.

Opinion Makers

Even within the field of science, we have become too fascinated with celebrities to respect true scientists. During the 1950s, Jonas Salk was a legitimate hero. He was brilliant and he was courageous. His advocacy for polio vaccination was not universally accepted. He needed strength of conviction to follow through on his research in the face of strong opposition. He needed strength of mind to create the vaccine he was willing to fight for. Today we revere celebrities, not scientists. Today, we go to Michael J. Fox to learn about Parkinson's disease. That is appropriate on a level. He is a well loved celebrity with a high profile. He gives a human face to a condition that our scientists need help fighting. We should not however, seek his opinions on stem cell research. He is not trained to give those opinions with the insight of an expert. It is possible to let a celebrity heighten our awareness about an issue, and then shift our focus to a member of the scientific community for greater comprehension.

The reason stem cell research is controversial is because certain doctors insist on harvesting stem cells from aborted fetuses. Stem cells may be classified in different ways. Some are totipotent, meaning that they may become any cell in your body. Those totipotent stem cells are completely undifferentiated. They are blobs of clay that have been completely untouched. They can become any type of cell: muscle, nervous, epithelial or connective.

If we do not employ totipotent stem cells from aborted fetuses for stem cell research, do we have other options? Yes. Pluripotent stem cells can become a variety of cell types. Think back to our one blob of clay analogy. Now compare 10 blobs of clay given to 10 different students in an art class. One student begins to make a sphere, but stops. Another begins to make a cube, another an oval, etc. etc. etc. Those blobs of clay are partly formed, but not fully formed. If they stop what they are doing and you want to create a project using one of their partially formed blobs, you have to first correctly select the primary form which has taken shape. If you wanted to make a ceramic basketball, take the clay shaped like a sphere. If you wanted to create a ceramic egg, take the clay shaped like an oval, a ceramic jack in the box, begin with the cube, etc.

To run with that analogy, we will discuss pluripotent stem cells further. These are partly formed stem cells, but not completely formed. Example: a hematopoietic stem cell gives rise to blood cells. A patient needing white blood cells can employ hematopoietic stem cells, as can a patient suffering from anemia and a diminished red blood cell count. In cases of neurological disease, neurons (the cells responsible for transmission of thought and nerve impulses) can not be used because they are post mitotic, meaning unable to reproduce. However support cells, such a glial cells of the nervous system, are mitotic. We can find sources of viable therapies while staying within the boundaries of ethical behavior.

It therefore makes sense to focus our energies on treatments available from adult stem cells. What has happened in the change from embryonic stem cells to adult stem cells is that the cells have transitioned from an ability to make any cell when they are a totipotent embryonic stem cell, to the ability to make certain specific cells as adult stem cells. This means they are stem cells that can be found in adults, and they have some programming done regarding their adult form. It is better to harvest stem cells from adults who have given permission, rather than dead fetuses. Here is where the significance hits hard, we have scores of available therapies that are linked to adult stem cells; why do we need to accept abortion as a human harvest field?

This is why we were better off placing Jonas Salk on a pedestal when discussing science, rather than a celebrity. Training people to listen to celebrities needs to be stopped. It is more important to have a willingness and an intellectual capacity sufficient to listen to people with clinical expertise, even if they are not as well known or attractive as those celebrities we love.

With stem cell research, there is an obstacle that, seems to be illogically thought of as an obstacle, the question of morals. When Barack Obama lifted the ban on federally funded research using embryos, he stated "Scientific decisions now will be made on facts, not ideology". A journalist named Kathleen Parker in her article "Obama ignoring the facts" made the point that you can be morally right and still be scientifically inclined. Ms. Parker went on to discuss the new desire to create embryos specifically to use them as experimental material. We are on a slippery slope, where the question of good and evil will be tested severely. Should we be willing to do what is morally wrong in scientific research? No. In fact, science should always be powered by a desire to do what is right. It is right to treat diseases, it is right to improve living conditions, it is right to care about the world and its inhabitants. Those ideals need no modification. Opposing the use of embryonic stem cell research take into account the idea that stem cell harvesting from a placenta is acceptable. After all, the placenta is not the baby. The afterbirth is yet another example of how we have access to cells for research while respecting human life.

A similar sequence regarding celebrities and science took place with the immunization as it relates to autism debate. Jenny McCarthy made endless appearances as an opponent of immunization. Such debates are highly interesting, yet when the media chooses to offer up a Playboy Bunny as the expert, there should be confusion as to why we are listening to scientific opinions from a person whose notoriety is based on appearing in such a magazine. That does not mean she is wrong or acting with bad intentions when advocating for clarity with regard to immunization and its risks. I saw her interviewed on the topic, she spoke well. She was genuinely concerned, and sincere in her efforts. I would just rather learn about science from a scientist, and I would prefer to see young women exposed to more women like Cokie Roberts or Doris Kearns Goodwin, who made names for themselves through intellectual endeavors.

TV as a Learning Tool

As expanding media outlets have created more specific audience niches within the broadcast field, people may chose to watch only those exact programs which cater to their primary taste. For those of you who are old, like me, you remember having about 8 selections of TV programs to choose from on the old dial of your TV with the rabbit ear antennas and channel knob. Having only eight channels to choose from meant that sometimes you were bored, and in trying to find something to watch, when "nothing good was on", you might have ended up watching a documentary on PBS.

After the feeling of dejection wore off over the fact that there was nothing better on, you found yourself paying attention and learning. You may have even thought that watching PBS was not so bad. In such a way, many people found they actually enjoyed learning. We have said good-bye to that era of television viewing, but gained something else.

Now we have programming twenty four hours per day highlighting science, nature, history, etc. That is great. However, people may also choose to spend twenty four hours per day watching adults fight over whose baby goes with which daddy or whose girl has cheated on whose husband with which cousin. That type of program, which could not get air time when there were only 8 channels needing material, is now also available twenty four hours per day. Television like any tool can be good or bad, it can be a great way to strengthen one's mind, and it can be a tool to poison one's soul. Despite the availability of 24 hour programming we still need some form of accountability for broadcasters.

Explaining biomes to a student who has once or twice watched a nature program is 10x easier than explaining them to a student with absolutely no prior exposure.

A desire to be the best in one's profession is surely an enticement to seek opportunities to strengthen one's mind. That is one of the difficult aspects of teaching. The teacher who surfs the web while kids do worksheets or who does online shopping while kids have a study hall in an academic class, is as well rewarded as the teacher who teaches every minute of class, stays late to help kids, grades homework and corresponds with parents. Being a great teacher is a good thing, but in certain schools an optional thing. This is all the more reason to respect quality teachers.

Why?

Giving students a solid foundation in the sciences empowers them to create and implement the technologies which will allow us to better use and conserve the precious resources essential to survival. Every day we see examples of situations that call for careful consideration and scientific approaches to problem solving. In looking at a traffic jam with thousands of cars lined up, wasting gas just to stand still, the first feeling might just be happiness to be going in the opposite direction; a second thought should be concern for all of that wasted fossil fuel. Public transportation needs to become more common in the United States, and cars with a higher fuel efficiency need to become more readily available. Recently, a few high school and middle school teams of future engineers made headlines by designing cars that can go hundreds of miles on a gallon of gasoline. The DeLaSalle car is one example. If a few students with a college professor or high school teacher as a mentor can create such vehicles, why is it that Detroit did not do so? The bailout money the auto industry received could have been tied to a requirement that they create such vehicles. Obviously the light weight materials necessary in construction would pose a safety concern for a real car. So why do we not have a car with even half of that fuel efficiency? The longer we wait to develop fossil fuel alternatives, the closer we come to a break in availability of energy. There is no reason to completely deplete our fossil fuel resources before addressing this problem. Fracking is a way of licking the bowl of fossil fuels dry while disrupting ground water supplies. A citizenry who consider all of the implications of the manner in which we use natural resources is more likely to accept slight inconveniences as a means of avoiding future hardships. We again return to the notion of schools as places where students learn such lessons.

The future problems we face will be problems requiring scientific knowledge; that knowledge should be found not only in the minds of the scientists, but also in the minds of the legislators who govern us, and the citizens who employ techniques to conserve and preserve our natural resources. If the United States chooses not to drill for oil in the Gulf of Mexico while Cuba grants drilling rights to Russia, China and Venezuela, is the environment any safer than if we joined the process? Do we lose potential revenue by not drilling for our own supplies? Why have we not yet created technologies to diminish our fossil fuel needs? Government needs scientists, and scientists need informed legislators.

It is wise to learn everything possible about every subject that can be studied, however, knowing scientific laws bridges gaps between peoples and cultures and generations. Songs change in popularity, styles change, favorite movies and books come and go, but objects still fall towards earth due to gravity. Fads are fleeting, scientific facts are perennial, we should give our attention to scientists even if Newton never danced to disco music, sported a mullet or let his pants droop mid-thigh (as far as we know).

CHAPTER SIX

Around the Horn

(A scientist's perspective on non-science classes)

"You wasted $150,000 on an education you coulda got for $1.50 in late fees at the public library."

~ Will Hunting

As Americans, it would be great to live in a country where being well educated, kind, hard working and honorable represents the norm. We often want to be special though and not normal. As the T-shirts says: "I am special and unique, just like everybody else". A child should know that they are special. If a child does not know that they already are special, they may go to great lengths to illustrate how special they are (hopefully in a good way). Other times, those behaviors may be offensive; kids may use foul language to demonstrate how rules do not apply to them. Sometimes, they act out in other ways. Often we make exceptions on reasonable expectations of behavior to exonerate offensive people on their quest to be "special". When we do that, we efface the idea that we can even have a "norm". There are more than enough ways to be special while still hoping that the definition of "normal" could be: to be well educated, kind and hard working.

We still have room to praise kids for the extra achievements they accomplish. With those basic qualities of goodness as a foundation, individuals can then go off in millions of directions regarding their individuality. Some will become great in sports, art, drama, writing or other endeavors. Being well educated, kind and hard working, will not hinder any other attributes a child may possess, but it is a great core set of character traits. In truth, there are no rules against just praising a kid for being nice.

There is more than enough for a teacher to master in trying to be the best possible teacher in their own classroom. That dedication to a single discipline should not eradicate their right to have opinions about what makes for a well rounded education.

Teachers in schools have their own role, just like members of a baseball team have their own role. The English teacher is specialized, but may have opinions about art. On a baseball team, the third baseman may have opinions about how to play left field. The third baseman's opinions about left field carry less weight than a left fielder's, but they come from a different perspective, and may provide insight.

Let's start our trip around the horn with history

History is one of the most important classes an American will take. We have a history based on high expectations, blessings gained via sacrifice and lofty ideals. That history we study has also, often been highly distasteful, even repugnant. We learn history not only to see role models of what is good, but also to remember what must never again be allowed to happen. Ensuring that younger students learn the names and places and events of history, allows college students to then analyze the causes and effects of those events.

John Adams upon the creation of the United States' form of government commented "Our constitution was made only for a moral and religious people. It is wholly inadequate to the government of any other." We can see today that he was right. As our values degrade, we begin to watch the fragmentation of a people, following the fragmentation of the families of those people. "Good time" behaviors are hard to argue against. Who does not want to have a good time? They are championed by people who do not look far into the future. These champions can never be hypocritical because their credo is: "Do whatever you want whenever you want". This credo may go off well enough for single people, but when children enter the picture, those children will need to be cared for.

A person who believes strongly in doing what they want when they want, will never be hypocritical. In contrast, a person who believes that right and wrong behaviors do exist may sin; they may act contrary to what they know to be true and correct. That person of values will then be vilified by the champions of good "times" as a hypocrite if they then take a stand contrary to their own behavior. Since it has been said: "All have sinned and fallen short of the glory of God", I do not believe we should ever lionize nor vilify a person, as we are all equally fallible. Our heroes may disappoint us. People we despise may make a good point, or a valuable contribution. Rather, we should rationally rate different behaviors, and be honest about the long term consequences of them and have values that are consistent with creating as harmonious a world as we can maintain. As we study history, we do not need to create flawless heroes, we can have flawed heroes who embody traits we wish to see in ourselves and our children. For the youngest children, we can focus on the best traits of our ancestors without always telling them the dirt.

So much of what we see in our historical figures and current leaders may lead to a degree of disillusionment. Alexander Hamilton's mea culpa when it was discovered that he had been unfaithful to his wife was the first major political scandal of our new republic. His confessing, rather than excusing his own behavior may make him seem to be a hypocrite.

If we do not become a "hypocrite nation", that is a nation where people own up to their own mistakes and dissuade repetition by younger generations, we will become a failed nation. The idea that "It's OK, I did it too", sets each of us up as the standard for an individualized system of morality. Things are not right or wrong based on whether we have or have not engaged in them. Since any imaginable behavior has been committed by someone, somewhere, our standards should not be so flexible as to fit all behaviors.

I once worked with a woman who was comfortable with drug abuse. She possessed great wisdom in her own mind. She was very clear in explaining that young people are going to use drugs and drink alcohol anyway, so she has them do it in her house where she can watch over them. A young man lost his life after he left a party at her house and crashed into a tree.

Positive Hypocrites

In contrasting her mindset with some former athletes who later in life started outreach programs to help younger athletes avoid pitfalls into which they themselves had fallen, we see examples of what I would call positive hypocrites. If a former player had a drug addiction and now works to help others recover from drug dependency or tries to help young players avoid the temptation to experiment with such chemicals, I would call such a person a positive hypocrite.

Race Issues in America

Let's look at an institution that was one of the greatest sins of our nation's history, the existence of slavery. In writing the Declaration of Independence, the clause Jefferson wrote, abolishing slavery was deleted by The Continental Congress. We could have started our existence free of that stain. Instead, to compromise with a few colonies, we allowed it to exist. Compromise is good when it comes to ordering pizza. If you want pepperoni, and your friend wants mushroom, buy plain. If compromise means you will go along with the abuse of millions of people as a means to an end, perhaps it is better to lose honorably than to cave in. The question is whether or not we could have won the revolution had we started as 10 original colonies turned into states, rather than 13. So how then has that grave offence played out?

Well, it is still playing out unfortunately. It should be a dead issue, and hopefully it soon will be. When Lincoln was soundly criticized for the great blood shed of the Civil War. His response, given in his second inaugural address was this:

"Woe unto the world because of offenses; for it must needs be that offenses come, but woe to that man by whom the offense cometh.' If we shall

suppose that American slavery is one of those offenses which, in the providence of God, must needs come, but which, having continued through His appointed time, He now wills to remove, and that He gives to both North and South this terrible war as the woe due to those by whom the offense came, shall we discern therein any departure from those divine attributes which the believers in a living God always ascribe to Him? Fondly do we hope, fervently do we pray, that this mighty scourge of war may speedily pass away. Yet, if God wills that it continue until all the wealth piled by the bondsman's two hundred and fifty years of unrequited toil shall be sunk, and until every drop of blood drawn with the lash shall be paid by another drawn with the sword, as was said three thousand years ago, so still it must be said 'the judgments of the Lord are true and righteous altogether".

During that war, over 600,000 white men died. When I was young, I internalized the guilt I'd been trained to absorb about racial inequality in America. Watching the videos of African Americans being sprayed with fire hoses, or watching the insults heaped on Jackie Robinson while viewing his biography cannot help but create a feeling of "white guilt" for an impressionable youth. As I have gotten older, the feeling of guilt for things I did not do, and crimes I did not commit has vanished. As a great great grandson of a soldier who fought for the Union during the Civil War. I now feel that, if I am to be equated with a white man who lived 150 years ago, why not the wounded warrior for freedom, from whom I am descended, rather than a random racist slave owner?

The truth is, no one in the twenty first century can claim the praise due one, nor the scorn due the other. We are accountable for our own behavior, and only with that mindset, can our country move forward. Each man and woman is accountable for only their own conduct. Still, as a nation, we can not forget our obligations to right our national wrongs. The key seems to be to let healing occur without continually reopening wounds.

Only through a deep understanding of our own history, can we come to such conclusions. If we do not think about the 2.5 million union soldiers who fought against slavery including the 360,000 who died, or the porters of the Underground Railroad, or abolitionists like William Lloyd Garrison and Harriet Beecher Stowe, it is possible to think of all antebellum white people in terms of lynch mobs or characters like Simon Legree.

When situations such as the Trayvon Martin case emerge, we see the residual effects of our history. Justice should be handed out in every situation whether it does or does not become a national news piece; it seems at times as though situations of injustice are used to stoke the flames of racial unrest so the news media can try to create riots that they will later cover. We saw that happen during the Rodney King case. When mobs became violent, victims were chosen because of their race and viciously beaten. We saw how the victims of senseless violence are rarely the people who were in any way involved in the incident that originally drew ire. Senseless violence can be directed towards any particular ethnicity depending on the circumstances.

The parable of the Good Samaritan is not merely a parable about a Jew and a Samaritan; it is a parable about any two people with different heritages who have been taught to hate each other. The lesson is that God does not care about ethnic groups, we are all taught to love each other.

The only way to truly eradicate racism is to focus solely on oneself. Always look people in the eyes. In the eyes, you see another human being. You do not see skin color, nose rings, tattoos, crazy hair or other superficial traits. It does not mean you will like everyone you meet, but you will see them as a person rather than a member of a group.

There was a time when reconciliation required government intervention. It is time to let the citizenry heal these wounds. The cessation of treating people like independent subgroups of citizens will lead to the acceptance of each other as fellow human beings. The way Pee Wee Reece showed his friendship with Jackie Robinson surely had a bigger impact than anything the government could have done during the early days of the civil rights era when we think about directly touching someone's heart.

It is much better to teach about Colin Powell when the curriculum covers recent American history than during Black History month. The first approach focuses on a man's achievements and contributions to America, clearing away the subject of race. The latter approach reinforces the notion of race as a factor in why we would study someone's achievements.

Having twice withdrawn from college for financial reasons as an undergraduate, it was impossible not to notice government efforts to rectify past injustices. I remember on one occasion sitting in the financial aid office, hoping to find a scholarship. Within the financial aid books, were scores of scholarships available to people of various persuasions. For almost all of them, I was ineligible because I am white or because I am male. There are people who died in the Civil War to end slavery, and there are people who faced lynch mobs, or who were sprayed with fire hoses for eating lunch at an integrated lunch counter. To me, fell the very easy task of paying for a college education by scrambling to save money and working whatever low paying menial task I could find, rather than being provided tuition money by a third party via scholarships or grants.

There was a time when, in order to balance the inequity still lingering from our past, race needed to be a factor in distribution of educational grants. That meant that for me, scholarship money was scarce. In the grand scheme of things, my burden was very light. It is now time to move away from an excessive focus on race. It is time to accept people on an individual, one by one basis.

People who have found a way to pay for their own education know it is possible, and know others can do the same. Certain good attitudes are borne with knowledge of history. History allows us to place minor inconveniences in contrast with actual hardships.

A woman named Mrs. Woinsky was my high school history teacher. She gave her students a gift of love for history. For people who love history, there are many great books to enjoy, such as *Alexander Hamilton* by Ron Chernow, *A Sorrow in Our Hearts* by Allan Eckert, *Lincoln* by David Donald, *The Autobiography of Frederick Douglass* and *Undaunted Courage* by Stephen Ambrose among many others. When you read about the struggles other people have faced and overcome, you become more comfortable with your own ability to overcome your own problems. At the very least, you become less likely to feel sorry for yourself. Not getting a pony for Christmas is not tragic for a person who has learned about The Khmer Rouge

Trials we encounter in our twenty first century lives will never compare to standing an over night watch at Valley Forge while wearing nothing but a blanket, and rags for shoes. Studying history gives us an insight into the realities of our own lives that we should gladly accept.

A failure to understand history has serious implications across the spectrum of issues for a nation of people who elect the president of the strongest country on earth. Perhaps a time will come when those words from this book will seem archaic "the strongest country on earth". How much longer will the United States of America be the strongest country on earth? Certainly our days in that role will be lessened if we do not become a country better able to educate and prepare young people to justify that statement.

Our current trajectory will have us fall significantly in the rankings of world leaders during our lifetimes should we fail to address the underlying causes for that trajectory. At the very minimum, a high school graduate should be able to pass the citizenship test administered to immigrants.

Daniel Helm

Opportunities and Second Chances

The great thing about our American education system is that we have community colleges. If for some reason a student did not have the chance to properly prepare themselves for a 4 year college during high school we have second chances. If a person cannot afford a four year school, we have alternatives. We should also have diplomas that indicate preparedness for trade school. Academics should never be snobs who fail to appreciate the special skills it takes to master mechanical trades.

Once, after stopping to help a stranded motorist who was in heavy traffic on the Garden State Parkway, I learned the young man was a student at Brown University (but he did not know how to change a flat tire). Clearly, an aptitude in book learning got him into that elite university. Just as clearly, that aptitude was not going to get him a job on Tony Stewart's pit crew.

There are news article which might fall into one of three categories: either intentionally misleading an ignorant populace, or written by an author lacking true historical perspective, or perhaps just having been said in a way that chooses not to specify facts with the belief that the reader already knows the basic facts. In these cases, we need an intelligent citizenship to correctly discern the implications of the article.

On April 9th, 2011, Donna Cassata of the Associated Press wrote an article about the funding Planned Parenthood receives from the federal government. It presented both sides in a fair and impartial manner. There was only one sentence that caught my eye, as possibly misleading. The article traced the funding for Planned Parenthood back to Title X, signed into law by President Nixon, a Republican. I felt that in doing so, the article left the reader believing that a desire to fund abortion on demand has at times, enjoyed bipartisan support.

The original intent of Title X was to provide health care to low income women. It was passed in 1970. Roe V. Wade occurred in 1973. Meaning that in 1970, no one would have thought they were creating a publicly funded system to finance abortion providers. A silly thing to focus on, but I often notice how small details are twisted or obfuscated, and wonder how other people perceive those incongruities.

When it comes to talking about abortion, the deep seated passions rise almost instantly. If you tell a person you are pro-life, you can surely expect an almost instant retort of: So you think rape victims should be forced to deliver the rapist's baby?! This type of retort ends discourse. If we want to reduce the amount of rape in our culture, we should be weeding from our culture the behaviors that lead to sexual assaults, beginning with our acceptance of perverse sexuality. Perverse sexuality is often glamorized in our culture, as it is in books like *Fifty Shades of Grey*. If a woman wants to be taken seriously in her stand on women's rights, she should be a loud opponent of what we accept in culture that leads to perversion.

From race relations to reproductive rights to international relationships to domestic issues and our tragic failure to make amends for the still continuing effects of "The Indian Wars", it is not enough that American students take history classes, they must understand American and world history, and feel a responsibility to take part in caring for our nation and our world.

Continuing around the horn, we come to elective courses

I took a middle school home economics class. A typical day might follow this pattern: we would arrive, there would be cooking materials available, we would cook something, eat it, then we would clean up.

One day for materials we had English muffins, Ragu sauce and mozzarella cheese waiting for us. This was a memorable activity because the big joke was to cut up a bar of soap and place the white cubes of soap into someone's mozzarella. English Muffin Pizzas do not taste good when made with soap, first hand experience speaking. We took the ingredients, made English muffin pizzas, ate them, then washed the dishes and left.

Such classes are a great diversion during the day. For the teacher of such a class, since there is no homework to grade, the hours are short and the work day ends when the kids leave. It can also be a class that a teacher takes seriously and uses as a platform from which to educate students about nutrition, etc.

Elective courses are a beloved part of any high school student's day, however, if we are going to stabilize the cost of education, consideration must be made for the type of preparation each staff member must go through before entering the classroom, and the time commitment each staff member needs to invest each day in order to complete their duties. Classes which do not generate homework to be graded can be linked with an extra duty period during the day. If one teacher receives two prep periods per day to grade homework and is grading homework during that time, while another teacher has two prep periods which are break periods, the second teacher could pick up a duty such as covering a lunch period or a study hall.

A great wood shop teacher not only prepares future carpenters, but also keeps repair costs for a school district manageable by fixing broken equipment, creating sets for the school play, and many other essential functions. Such a teacher has great value to a school district. There are also shop teachers who let kids play ping pong every day before sending out grades of "A" on the report card. The problem being that a young person does not realize that the teacher who provides free hang out time is receiving the same salary as the teacher who is providing an education. While there may be courses which let students catch their breath during the day (no one wants to take calculus 8 periods per day) those courses should still be offering the students something enriching.

The link between high math scores and a student's ability to read music tends to stop opponents of music programs from complaining too loudly about the expense of these programs.

Elective courses have great value, but there will be many debates to come as the use of standardized testing works its way into teacher evaluations because not every course is tested in such ways. If standardized test scores are going to be linked with retention of employment, there is a distinct disadvantage to being employed in a discipline which is thus scrutinized, therefore, there will need to be some system in place to balance the compensation for different teachers.

Next stop: English class

The first adult book I read cover to cover was the biography of Constantine. I was home sick for a few days, I was bored, and the book was in our house, so I read. Young people today do not have the burden of being bored, they have thousands of dollars in home electronics to keep them preoccupied with hour after hour of mindless entertainment.

Considering the concept of minutes and hours of our lives as currency, that mindless expenditure of currency can be compared to a coin operated game, the one with a crane and a claw. The items in the display are all too heavy to be held by the claw, so a child puts quarter after quarter into the machine and after spending their last quarter, the child is left with nothing.

Constantine was not a book I would have picked to read on my own. It just happened to be in the house. My selection was limited, which was fortunate. The book was educational and entertaining. English teachers should not give students free range of what they choose to read. There are too many students writing book reports on Eminem and Justin Bieber. If a young person wants to read such books they should do so on their own time, an English teacher should not legitimize such choices as educational experiences.

All English teachers should create book lists that cover a wide array of tastes while staying within the bounds of legitimate literature. Many of the older teachers stick with that policy, while younger teachers sometimes choose to be more hip (not that "hip" means hip anymore, but you get the idea). A student is better off being given a hand-out with a list of books such as Great Expectations, The Autobiography of Frederick Douglass, Killer Angels, Uncle Tom's Cabin, Little Women, The Grapes of Wrath and the like on it, rather than being told that the biography of R Kelly is literature. On the list, the teacher can put a summary of each book, then let the students choose which they will select. By keeping a closet full of such books, they can be a type of librarian. (Better yet, use the school library.) The value of school libraries is being lost in the internet age. A quiet corner with a good book and a soft chair is a great thing.

Some people criticize teachers for using the same materials year after year, it is wrong to criticize them. The same list can effectively be reused in English class year after year. (Edgar Allan Poe will not be writing anything new this year.)

It is not the material that needs to be replaced yearly. It is the teacher's approach to their new group of students that will be reappraised on a yearly basis. Teachers will learn which student needs what type of help, which student struggles where. It is the approach to each individual person that is regularly refreshed, not Shakespeare.

Get on your sweats, and watch out for wedgies in the locker room. Time for gym!

Gym class is one of those classes where kids can just be happy. Obviously, exercise is the purpose, however it is a fun purpose.

"When I was 5 years old my mother always told me that happiness was the key to life. When I went to school, they asked me what I wanted to be when I grew up. I wrote down "happy". They told me I didn't understand the assignment, and I told them they didn't understand life" ~ John Lennon

There are great phys ed. teachers out there, and there are people who roll out a bunch of basketballs, then hang around until the dismissal bell rings while reading a newspaper.

Creating healthy individuals is the most important part of sports, and yet there is also a component of mental development involved as students learn rules and strategies for the different games. Physical Education done right, is a combination of boot camp and a half time chalk talk. The students are being physically and mentally challenged while enjoying the social aspect of activities.

Despite the importance of physical education, student athletes should not have to take a gym class when their sport is in session. Student athletes regularly practice from 3:00 until 6:00. A winter athlete may be competing from 7:00pm until 9:00pm with a bus getting home from an away game at 10 pm or later. I have had students tell me they did not complete their homework until 2 or 3 am. We are not doing these kids justice by having them keep such schedules. Homework is an important component in a quality education. Students who succeed in college know how to handle the responsibility of completing homework. Still, when an athlete's sport is in season, it would be nice for the student to have less homework (at least, less homework that they need to do at home). A study hall should replace gym class for in-season athletes.

Many kids today have too many outside obligations. If time for homework is not available because of a commitment to a recreational team on top of the school team, the recreational team must be the first thing dropped. Homework should never be in question. If students are not completing 1 to 2 hours of homework nightly, they are not learning the habits required to succeed at the college level. In cultures where students go to school 11 months per year, less homework is logical. In the United States, we have 2 months of summer vacation. We need a more rapid pace between September and June if we are to keep pace with the rest of the industrialized world. While physical education is an important part of a child's school day, it is redundant for in-season athletes and they should be exempted from it.

Parlez-Vous Francais? Oui un peu, parce que j'ai etude Francais pour trois annees

Most Americans will study a foreign language for 4 to 6 years so we can learn to say: "I speak a little French" or "I speak a little Spanish". We are particularly adept at coupling such a phrase with quizzical stares when a foreigner then responds in the language we just used.

Regarding foreign languages, our main problem is that we do not follow the cognition sequence of infants when we learn a foreign language. We are interested in teaching grammar to children who lack a single word of vocabulary. Repetition and familiarity are important keys early in the developmental process. Rather than focus on moving on from lesson one to lessons two, three, etc. we should observe small children learning a language. They will have a favorite show, and watch it over and over.

The first time, a student hears:

"Comment allez vous?"

"Je suis tres bien, merci, et vous?"

"Je suis d'accord"
They may only understand a few words within the conversation, although, they can understand the gist of the conversation. In order to more effectively advance from that point, to proficiency, they require repetition. It is not fair to make an entire class keep the pace of the slowest student so that all may achieve proficiency. For that reason, the investment in audio labs for schools is an important expense that should not be ignored. When students have access to such labs during their study hall time, they may advance themselves via a sufficient amount of personally invested time. At that point, a student who is not keeping pace with the class will earn a lower grade, yet the instructor can feel comfortable that the path to success was left open and materials were made available to the student.

Due to the rate at which we receive immigrants into this country, it is understandable that some Americans feel we should not have to learn a second language to be literate within our own borders. No sign should ever be written in another language, unless that sign is first written in English, and has a second or more languages provided beneath the English. I know that when I travel abroad, it is a relief to see a sign written in English. We should extend the same courtesy to our foreign guests. I believe people who oppose the notion of accepting other languages domestically, would feel more comfortable with such accommodations in our country if English was declared the official language of the United States.

Now to expand on some people's argument that an American should not have to learn a foreign language just because we often have non-English speaking visitors is to accept that the reverse must also be true. We would need to learn the language of the countries we visit. When I am abroad, and I see an irate American speaking English louder and more slowly to a native in his own country; I know that I am looking at an adult who spent his or her youth demanding that foreigners coming to America learn English. As Steve Martin says: "When I travel to a foreign country, I expect they would have had the common courtesy to learn English."

When I travel, I have always found people to be amazingly kind to me, as I struggle with their language. I think part of that has to do with the fact that I am willing to struggle with their language. When people know you are making an effort, they will travel far beyond half way to meet you.

When my ship left San Diego after refresher training, and resupplied before going through the Panama Canal, we stopped in Costa Rica. It was absolutely gorgeous, and the people could not have been kinder. During one exchange, when I was trying to communicate with a cashier, her patience was saintly. There was a look of concentration on her face, as she navigated my Spanish gibberish, and that concentration was endearing. She finally understood me, and I purchased some souvenirs. There were some small children there who were laughing at my attempts. It was a joyful laughter devoid of a hint of mocking or cruelty. Surely, they just enjoyed an adult speaking like a three year old, and could not help giggling. It is a memory that always comes to mind when I encounter a foreigner in America. I want to show them the same level of patience and kindness that a Costa Rican would.

On another occasion, I was mocked for foreign language deficiencies, yet even that amused me. While visiting Stockholm, Sweden, I wanted to order lunch. Imagine looking at a menu board, without understanding a thing. Finally, I asked a waitress: "Vad ar bra?" She looked very puzzled at me. I am pretty sure I was asking: "What is good?" After a few more unsuccessful attempts, I confessed: "Jag talar Svenska intebra." And inquired: "Talar du Engelska?" (I speak Swedish poorly. Do you speak English?) She helped me place an order, Swedish meatballs and noodles. It was a great meal. While eating, some young men on the other side of the restaurant began looking at the menu and asking each other: "Vad ar bra?" (With my accent) It was the type of thing where, even being the butt of the joke, you have to admit it was funny.

It would help American schools to initiate a program where we regularly recruit and trade teachers with other countries, exposing our children to as many native speakers as possible. Schools would be well served to have at least one foreign born member of their foreign language faculty at any time. It would be difficult logistically, but we surely have enough educators willing to travel abroad to make such swaps possible.

The opinions of a science teacher on other subjects will naturally be biased, and can only be offered with less authority than those who have mastered those other subjects. When a baseball team, following a put out, throws the ball around the horn as little more than a team bonding exercise, so it was that this chapter was a way to tip my hat in appreciation to other educational professionals while sharing the opinions accrued over a 20 year teaching career.

CHAPTER SEVEN

Special Education, a Growing Concern

The federal Individuals with Disabilities Education Act provides a set of protections for 6.6 million students—about 13 percent of total student enrollment—who have dyslexia, autism, intellectual disabilities, blindness, or other impairments that affect educational performance. Those students are entitled to a "free, appropriate public education" in the least-restrictive environment that meets their needs. Fail to provide such services, and parents can sue in federal court.

~ Christina A. Samuels

In basketball, not everyone can dunk the basketball. If you are coaching a team, rather than frustrate yourself and your athletes by trying to teach everyone to dunk, teach some to pass well, others to be good three point shooters, and others to be strong defensive players. Of course, if you want everyone to be able to dunk, you can lower the net so there is no challenge to the feat. This is where special education can lose its true purpose. Some people want to lower standards so everyone can reach the goal. Other people want to try and force kids to do what they cannot do. The best solution is to find where each child can excel, and then teach them how to excel in that area. There is no need to ignore areas where the child is weak, it won't hurt a child to try hard and earn a C. One of the biggest weaknesses in providing special education support to students lies in the fact that it is easier to change a grade of 60 to 70 by erasing the 6 and writing a 7, than it is to spend 2 hours with a student helping them understand a concept with greater clarity. Do people actually change grades out of complacency to meet goals? Yes they do. The other options as stated are to spend a great deal of time helping a student reach such goals, accept that they will score lower in certain areas or increase staffing. Increasing staff increases expenses, which are already rising. "Over the past 10 years, the number of U.S. students enrolled in special education programs has risen 30 percent." (nea.org/specialed)

The questions are: Why are those enrollments rising, and how do we address the needs? I have had experiences where working with a child for an hour or more every week allows them to catch up to where they needed to be to succeed in a high school. If time can reduce the number of classified students, time needs to be spent.

Special Education is the only department in a school building capable of influencing every other department. Those influences can be very bad. On one occasion, after reporting a boy, with no cognitive deficiencies, for calling a female teacher the most vulgar litany of names I've ever heard from a student to a teacher, it became clear that special education has the ability to cause severe damage to American schools. Despite his lacking the cognitive deficiencies that special education exists to work with, I was informed that he has a behavioral disability and "impulse control" is part of that disability. He received no punishment for the incident. This gives us the following list of disabilities a special education teacher must contend with: dyslexia, hearing impairment, visual impairment, autism, ADHD and of course, the tendency to call a woman every form of vulgarity under the sun.

Special education budgets need to be minimized and those minimized resources need to be used more effectively by providing them exclusively to students with legitimate needs. It does not mean that students with issues that fall outside of the realm of medically based issues are to be ignored. Many needs currently addressed by special education could be addressed by the type of mentoring that occurs when teachers care enough about their students to sit with them and have a conversation. Well timed vignettes of concern in a teacher/student relationship are often of much greater value than orchestrated interventions done in accordance with state regulations, although there are times when those more formal interventions are needed. These types of interludes have, not accidentally, been discouraged in recent years. Teachers are told to only speak with students in open areas, or in classrooms with open doors. There is a taboo about one on one conversations with students. This is because you can no longer go one month without seeing a news story about a teacher who had a sexual relationship with a student. This is again due to the degraded morals in a country that chooses to worship sexuality while ignoring personal responsibility and self control. It is a case where responding to a wrong, prevents a right. If an adult cannot be trusted to sit and talk with a student, they should not be in education.

The essence of education for a child with learning disabilities is the same as the essence of educating a child who is not in a special education class. Find the area where that child is special and gifted. Cater to their strengths while chipping away at their weaknesses. Do not look at their weaknesses as an excuse for those students to offer less effort than any other student. Not every student can solve a calculus problem, but every student can exert their best effort. Often the trick is to find what most interests the child.

Does a child love the ocean and sailing? Give them Moby Dick for their reading assignment. Do they love cars? Teach them chemistry by working on the reactions within an internal combustion engine. Explaining the process of combustion will tie chemistry in to a car's need for a carburetor. The carburetor mixes the fuel with the air. Students can write and balance the formula for octane reacting with oxygen, then producing carbon dioxide and water. Balancing a chemical equation can be tricky. It is possible to make it more interesting by tying it in with something the student likes. Keep in mind that some special education students have spent their entire academic careers being told they cannot do this or that. It is good to show them what they can do. It is not possible to cater to every student in this way, but it is possible after having had a conversation with a student who is struggling to be cognizant of their needs. Since the whole class is going to learn how to balance an equation anyway, why not give that one student an added boost by making the lesson revolve around their favorite topic of interest?

There seems to be two broad groups of special education teachers. One group exerts every effort to help a student overcome their area of difficulty. They bring honor to the profession. Another group constantly leans on the excuse that the child is incapable of X, Y and Z, and therefore, must not be held accountable for any of it. The latter group may give answers to a student during testing, or provide passing grades regardless of work quality and effort, or may simply have the child do nothing all semester, then place a passing grade on the report card. The group that helps a child learn often finds that a special education student soon becomes capable of handling college prep courses. The fact that only 4% of special education students are ever reclassified out of special education is data to address.

The teachers who give away free passing grades often make everybody happy. The parents are happy that their child is passing, the student is happy to be passing and the teacher leaves at the end of the student school day, having done nothing, but still receiving the same paycheck as the teacher who stays four hours longer and works every minute from 7am until 6pm. The former teacher is rare. They still have compassion, and find ways to help a student pass the course, even if the course is very challenging. They hold the child accountable for making an effort and meeting standards appropriate for the child's ability level. In this way, the student acquires knowledge, but more important, the child develops a work ethic. They feel and should feel proud of what they have done. When they find employment, they will strive to do well, and ask for help if needed, but still place expectations on themselves. Students who move on from a low quality teacher have learned to demand lower expectations from those around them. They believe it is the job of others to accept less.

There are a great many laws regarding how schools implement special education modifications, however, being legally accountable is less valuable than touching a child's heart and changing his or her direction in life. It is very rare that a school is not in compliance with special education regulations. However, compliance does not guarantee success for the child. In the October 2010 edition of *Educational Leadership*, Buffum, Mattos and Weber presented alarming statistics regarding special education students. "According to the U.S. Department of Education, the graduation rates of students with special needs is 57%". Along with that data, they shared that it is estimated that 50% of prison populations are made up of former special education students, and only 4% of classified students will ever be redesignated. My experience with special education students has shown me that when they are held to high standards, and assisted in meeting those high standards, they succeed. The incarceration rate is an alarming statistic. It is a personal opinion that we, as a nation, are too greatly limiting employment opportunities when we choose to ship unskilled labor off-shore. Some people are not academically gifted. We are creating an economy where they are therefore unemployable and more likely to turn to crime. Being willing to work should be a sufficient entry level qualification.

In "In Class Support" classes, a special education teacher and a subject area teacher will work together in a class where regular education students and special education students are mixed. It is expected that no student knows who in their class has special needs. Still, it is not a secret when students see another student receiving help beyond what they receive, or a different test, plus, kids talk. Sometimes the regular education kids will want the accommodations being provided to the special education kids. Restructuring the in class support model, and having the students during class truly treated equally is the answer, then giving the student with special needs one additional study hall period per week where they can receive more specialized instruction would more effectively meet the student's needs. Paying two teachers to always be together in the same class when one is sufficient becomes wasteful. With that one extra study hall, special education students can receive math help Monday, history help Tuesday, etc. This would be preferable for many special education teachers as well, often they would rather be busy instructing children than watching another teacher teach. It only requires a few periods per week for the special education teacher to keep up with what is happening in class. One extra day of instruction per class, coupled with testing modifications would be sufficient if the student was truly ready for an inclusion class. If they are not, a replacement class would be the best alternative.

The key with special education is to be an advocate for strengthening the student's skill set rather than making excuses and enabling a student to put forth less than their best effort. I never minded running behind my daughter, holding her bike while she peddled as she learned, but the goal was to get her into a position where the support was no longer needed. These opinions are personal opinions and were not developed through extensive controlled studies, therefore it is not my intention to overstep my bounds into the realm of the professionals in this field. It is however from first hand experience that I know some students who were being considered for treatment with medication but instead responded to extra attention, patience and encouragement.

CHAPTER EIGHT

Sex Education in a Modern Gomorrah

"In 2008, teen pregnancy and childbirth accounted for nearly $11 billion per year in costs to U.S. taxpayers for increased health care and foster care, increased incarceration rates among children of teen parents, and lost tax revenue because of lower educational attainment and income among teen mothers."

~ National Vital Statistics Report

> "It's a gift I want to give to my husband. Harder than training for the Olympics has been staying a virgin before marriage. If you marry me, then...yeah"
> ~ Lolo Jones, Olympic Athlete

There are things going on in our country that are worthy of great concern in the area of teen sexuality, so I wanted to start on a bright note. Lolo Jones, an Olympic athlete who looks like a model, made that statement on intimacy. She is a woman who deserves the utmost respect. We are fortunate to have such role models for the young ladies of today.

Headlines associated with education today seem, lately, to be connected as much with sexual impropriety as any other aspect of life in the classroom. We should not be surprised at the degree of sexual impropriety in our schools, although, we should be enraged by it. Teachers are the people who have a responsibility to instill a sense of safety in our children while those children go about the process of learning. Why should we not be surprised by the levels of sexual impropriety amongst teachers? Teachers are drawn from the same pool of people as every other profession; they are drawn from the citizenry of the country they inhabit. America is very comfortable with perversion. Teachers are drawn from the same pool of people as the Abu Ghraib prison guards who enjoyed sexually humiliating their captives. They are drawn from the same pool of people who spend 13 billion dollars per year on pornography. When I drive down the street in one section of my town, my goal is to avert my daughters' eyes from the Condom store with mannequins in the display window who are engaged in S & M activity. On the other side of town is the porn shop with a flashing sign advertising vibrators. We must stop the progress of accepting perversity as part of a "healthy sex life".

Over a decade ago, while leading a group of 6th graders on a tour of Provincetown Massachusetts, when we had some free time before a whale watching cruise, I allowed the chaperones to take the kids into some shops to purchase souvenirs. Having warned the chaperones that some stores seemed shady and that they should carefully monitor which stores the children entered, we departed in small groups. As I roamed the shopping area checking in on the student groups, I came upon a chaperone without his students.

"Where are your kids?" I asked.

"They are in this store, they told me to wait outside." He responded.

Upon entering the store, what I saw disgusted and disturbed me in numerous ways. The store had children's toys in the front, and then behind a partition with no means of restricting entry, sat a cove of filth that was beyond repulsive, and there in the midst of it stood the group of 11 year olds I was looking for.

I yelled for all of them to get out immediately. One girl asked if she could buy the juggling sticks she had picked up in the front. I said: "We are buying nothing here!" The 20 year old girl who sat behind the counter watching the destruction of innocence, said at that point: "Oh the prude". What kind of world have we generated when a young woman will let small children peruse such filth? Therein lies another problem. We can no longer hope that women espouse values born of a desire to defend children. The equality we sought as a society has not been achieved at the higher level of moral expectations women once defined. It has been achieved at the level a negative stereotype of sailors on leave once defined.

I believe it helps society when women expect men to conduct themselves in honorable ways.

For my bachelor party, I asked my brother to take me to a baseball game or a comedy club. My group of friends went to a comedy club. We had a great time. Afterwards, we went to a restaurant/bar for some drinks. When a woman learned we were a bachelor party, she offered to undress in the bathroom for me.

"No, that's fine but thank you," was perhaps an unexpected reply. She looked at me like I had two heads.

A friend of mine named Mark did the same thing during his bachelor party. We merely gathered for dinner as a group in a private back room of a restaurant. When our waitress offered herself as entertainment, he politely declined. It is good to befriend people you respect. Later, the woman at my bachelor party continued chatting with some friends of mine, mentioning that she had no idea where her 12 year old son was at that time (1 am), "probably getting into trouble" she added. Of course he is getting into trouble. He has no one to raise him.

We are in many regards fortunate to have the problems we have. Within our borders, mothers do not weep because their baby died when their home was bombed by a drone. The woman I mentioned from my bachelor party could very easily stay home, help her son do his homework then go to bed after watching a movie.

Again, in working with children as a teacher, the goal is not to condemn a student's parents to that child, but rather to be an unapologetic advocate for right behaviors. To say that children are best off when mom and dad are both working hard to take care of their children is a positive affirmation of what is right without being a direct condemnation of anyone in particular. To tell a student that a good education coupled with a commendable work ethic builds future opportunities, is again, advocacy for what is right while being a condemnation of nothing. If the boy who was out at 1 am while his mom was hanging out in a bar was in my class, I would have no right to criticize his mom, but I would want to advocate to him that he adopt habits which will lead to success in life. There would most likely be signs of what his upbringing was like, those signs are a good indication to spend some time giving the child encouragement and help with his studies.

A culture which accepts dysfunction as normal creates an increased need for government intervention in people's lives. On a personal level, I am willing to work two or three jobs in response to my family's needs, and more than happy to distribute money to people with financial hardships. Donations from private pockets anonymously given to a family in need, helps to meet their needs, and earns gratitude which, being undirected, may in the future be paid forward. Money from the government on a regular basis is seen as a right and an entitlement. Needing help at some point in one's life is not a terrible thing, but it is more important that the government provide people with an economy in which opportunities exist, rather than government assistance to survive an economy that does not provide opportunity.

Advocating for honorable lifestyles does not need to be drudgery, nor does it need to be unprofitable. Network executives perhaps need to be reminded that shows like The Cosby Show, Little House on the Prairie, and The Waltons had steady dependable viewers. It is not necessary to parade dysfunction as a way to draw viewers while satiating their hunger for titillation. Who we accept as appropriate role models is as much a function of what we saturate society with as what we praise.

Public figures have a difficult task, living their lives in the fish bowl of public opinion. More should learn to say: "I screwed up. I am sorry". A former politician, while in the midst of resigning as governor of New Jersey, in a frenzied effort to gain some degree of historical significance, grasped at the straw of homosexual firsts. He chose not to resign as a politician under investigation for misconduct, but as our nation's first openly gay governor.

I do not see where that act helped him or hurt him, but there can be no question that when sexual indiscretions ruin families, the children suffer. It is this pattern of physical pleasure without commitment that plagues America, putting schools in the untenable position of trying to compensate for poor parenting in the lives of too many children. Unless a person is prepared to commit his or her life to another person, dating, hand holding, and kissing, needs to be the standard people advocate for when young people are in a dating relationship. Wanting to know about a high school student's personal life is often tied to prurient curiosity, and should be avoided. When students confide in a trusted adult, that trust should be honored, but when speaking to a class, sticking with generalities and morally sound choices is the appropriate route.

Celebrating Success

The idea of "better or worse" is easily said, but much harder to live. It would be nice to give as much attention to couples who celebrate a 40th or 50th anniversary as we give to the misfortune of celebrities and their families when marriages disintegrate. Rather than look forward to reading about the inevitable consequences of what is wrong in a celebrity's relationships; we should praise and recognize the fruits of what is good in relationships. How did those couples with 50 year marriages do it? Hopefully, in situations where families collapse, the children rebound, however, in such situations the families can in no way be replaced by any mechanisms a school system can offer.

Straight forward sex education, without feeling a responsibility to make every possible sexual behavior acceptable should be the standard approach to sex education in schools. Young people will make up their own minds on the trajectory of our culture. With that in mind, morality based values need to be welcome in schools. Students should know the anatomy and physiology of the two reproductive systems. They should understand pregnancy and development, etc. When school districts start incorporating anal sex lessons in the curriculum for fifth graders, or have former prostitutes receive pay to come in as a guest speaker, they have greatly overstepped the legitimacy of their mandate. Both of those examples are drawn from real life.

What is happening in the arena of sexuality is more important than what is happening in any other area of our culture because, whether we like it or not, sex is the means by which children enter this world. It seems silly to state the painfully obvious as if presenting the solution to an esoteric mystery. However, if we emphasized the fact that sex leads to babies, we would not be telling high school kids: Sex is a natural, normal part of life and there is nothing wrong with having sexual relations at your age. Instead, we would ask them: Are you prepared to enter the work force in a full time capacity? Do you have your education completed? Are you comfortable making a life long commitment to another person? If not, it is only a few years until you are trained in a job or out of college and ready for that phase of your life. An adult's inability to force a young person to accept good advice should not preclude him or her from offering it.

The reality is that the days of getting married at 16 and dying at 45 are over; whether young adults do or do not accept the reality that it will be a couple of years, (not a decade), before they are prepared to settle into a sexual relationship, does not change the fact that it is the right message to share with them. Prior to that, they should go on dates, hold hands, kiss good night, but by no means should they be acting as if they could take care of a child. Neither should we be telling them that with proper precautions, pregnancy will not occur until they want it to occur. The use of precautions is an appropriate part of sex education, but it does not need to be presented as a green light.

Ultimately, the natural system seems like a pretty good system. One female and one male are required for conception and then you have two parents in place. They are similar in some ways, different in other ways, teamed up to provide a stable environment for the child. It is not more complicated than that. Of course, one of the greatest parts of the system is also the reason for the problems we face. It is pleasurable. When we adopt an *anything goes* mentality because sex is pleasurable, problems will be created. If we can tell people to enjoy alcohol responsibly, we can do the same for sex. In the case of sex, marriage is a good idea when it comes to responsibility.

I happen to be a big fan of Japanese dumplings called gyoza. However, I never craved them before enjoying one. Why rush kids into a relationship that will only leave them craving more, when they are not ready financially or emotionally? Let them enjoy their youth and the innocent affections they feel for the people they find attractive (but will, most likely, not marry). Later they can enjoy all the intimacy of a marital relationship when they are ready for all the responsibility and self sacrifice it entails. For now, let them pass notes, hold hands and go to movies together, and if they do not see that as a viable system for a relationship at their age, let's tell them it is. Their hormonal urges are strong forces, our advice can either encourage them towards free reign or self control.

Marriage can be a long haul. A friend of mine liked to say that he and his wife had been married for 5 years, but it felt like 5 minutes. After the women in the room delightedly sighed awwww, he would throw in "under water".

There is a joke about an Amish man's first visit to the big city. He and his son sat in the lobby of a fancy hotel, trying to understand all the new fangled gadgets they were seeing for the first time. Having never seen an elevator, and having no idea what it does, they were curious to see someone use the contraption. After a couple of minutes, an old woman very similar to the man's wife entered the elevator. The man and his son watched the doors close, and waited. One minute later, the doors reopened, and a gorgeous young woman stepped out. The old man looked at his son and said: "Go get your mother".

Marriage is not a day at the carnival, there are a lot of challenges to overcome. The people who benefit the most from healthy marriages are the children. They say it is wrong to keep a bad marriage together "for the children", and so it is. Therefore it makes sense to not let the marriage get bad in the first place. "Loving" your spouse is at times, not about feeling that emotion, it is about making that decision. If loving your spouse is contrary to some of the behaviors in our current culture, then it is good to be contrary to our current culture.

Cultural Paradigm Shift

Men no longer sense the responsibility to have honorable intentions with women, and women can now enjoy the indifference that some men have long enjoyed regarding sexual relationships. Men were the ones who, stereotypically, looked to use and discard sexual partners while creating a list of conquests legitimizing their claim to being a "real man". Some women now have also adopted the mentality that they are the ones with the sexual power to use and discard sexual partners. Sex in the City has done a lot to spread that message, but it began appearing during Madonna (Louise Ciccone)'s time as a pop queen.

Unfortunately, new times have not changed the reality that following a sexual tryst, it is the women left trying to fend for themselves and a child (or dealing with the emotional scars of having had an abortion). When promiscuity follows the road portrayed in countless movies and TV shows: there is no child, no STDs, just two contented people who have been pleasured, then gone on their happy ways. TV is not reality.

Daniel Helm

Role Models?

In that TV and celebrities influence children, their actions bear scrutiny. One highly publicized tragedy for a celebrity was the result of behaviors that the celebrity had championed. Before that celebrity faced the results of her own behaviors, she had advocated for the behavior to millions of kids. The death of Amy Winehouse occurred on July 23rd 2011. It is sad to lose a talented young woman. This sad event can be looked at from the perspective of those who knew and loved the young woman. It can also be looked at from the perspective of a person living in a society where uncounted millions of people die in anonymity each year from drug abuse. When young people start playing with drugs, they have thrown away their chance to be in control. By never trying them, a person has acknowledged that drugs are addictive and dangerous. A person who has never touched drugs keeps control of whether or not drugs will have a chance to control their life.

Discussing celebrities and their effect on society is unavoidable. However, some of the best examples celebrities set, are set outside of the public spotlight. When Tippi Hedren was asked about being pushed out of the movies by sexual harassment, her response was that the behavior ruined her career, but not her life.

In the case of Amy Winehouse, she chose to roll the dice, she was an advocate for a poor choice (drug abuse), yet she still was functioning as she spread that message. Here are her lyrics: "They tried to make me go to rehab but I said 'no, no, no', I ain't got seventy days, Cause there's nothing, There's nothing you can teach me".

That message is poured into millions of young people's minds. As a teacher, I deal directly with 100 to 150 young people every year. I know my influence on them is limited to being one of eight teachers during one of their 13 plus years in school. Still, a teacher will care about each and every one of their students and want to see them achieve success in their lives to the best of their ability. For that reason, any sadness over the loss of Amy Winehouse is offset by the hope that the reality of her death will send a message to children that her songs denied. If her death saves the life of an impressionable youth it was not a wasted death.

Returning to the topic of this chapter, 80% of unmarried teen girls who become pregnant are left before the baby is even born. Bristol Palin had her time in the spotlight as a famous pregnant teen. Her celebrity status (Dancing with the Stars) creates the false impression that the results of unwanted teen pregnancies are positive. In real life, young ladies do not become celebrities when they become pregnant, they struggle, their children struggle, and it leaves the whole of society struggling to help.

A woman who did a beautiful job broaching the issue of celebrity misdirection was Kathie Lee Gifford. When others were gloating over Lindsay Lohan's descent, Gifford made the following comment: "I can't help but think of Lindsay Lohan as that adorable little girl I interviewed when she did the parent trap". That is a positive perspective. Kathie focused on Lindsay's humanity and intrinsic worth. It is a focus on the possibilities of youth. It is a focus on the value of her as a human being.

Any of us, when taking a group of children hiking in the woods would make a point of showing them what poison ivy looks like, we would tell them to avoid it. We should approach harmful behaviors like any other danger, and point them out in the same way that we point out poison ivy, without worrying that we will offend some poison ivy anti-defamation league. A big part of our downfall as a society is linked to organizations like NAMBLA who try to legitimize assaults on innocence.

There are so many factions in our society that we can no longer advocate for wholesome lifestyles without being opposed by someone. Doing what is right while being applauded is good. Doing what is right while being opposed is far more difficult.

If we seek to resurrect our culture, we must be sensitive to moments like the 2011 teen choice awards. Ashton Kutcher received an award for "Friends with Benefits". The movie is a comedy about two people who decide to be sexual partners with absolutely no true commitment to each other. Receiving an award from teens means the teens liked the movie. Hence, they were introduced to the concept of uncommitted polyamory at a very impressionable age.

When this is what teens are absorbing via the culture, adults can not be wishy-washy about always trying to see both sides of an issue. Just say it is wrong. Hollywood often gets a bad reputation. That is because it often deserves a bad reputation.

Many times, celebrities embrace pernicious, trendsetting behaviors which are harmful to those who follow. Other times, we see in celebrities the frailties to which we are all susceptible. To this day, I am saddened by the death of Karen Carpenter. There are pressures young ladies feel to be some version of perfection which is unattainable. In Karen Carpenter's death, we see how a woman who embodied so much of what is good, kind and noble in humanity can, despite possessing physical beauty as well, still feel she somehow needs to be a better version of what she is. Teachers and other adults should not let an opportunity to say a kind word go unused. If we see something noteworthy from a young person, we should give them a pat on the back. Acknowledge what is good in them.

I have been asked by a friend if it is tough to be a teacher and be around all of those "hot" teenage girls with the way they dress. I answered no, they are kids. When you are around the kids all day, it does not cross your mind whether or not they are attractive. You do not see them in that way. They are not a collection of body parts. Each child has a name, a personality, and you see them as a person. You wish for each of them a happy future, a successful marriage, and an enjoyable career. In every kid you see good qualities, and you just hope that they see in themselves the goodness of which you are aware. Insecurity is one of the worst openings around, with which people that have bad intentions may snag their prey. An insecure child is vulnerable in ways a more secure child is not vulnerable. That goes for boys as well as girls. I believe that for teachers it is important to try and attend one of each freshman, JV and varsity competition each sports season. Teachers should go to students' theater presentations, their art shows, etc. then make a point of complimenting the kid who perhaps is not well known to their classmates. Praise in public, criticize in private. Build self esteem at all possible moments.

This diversion from the topic of this chapter may seem incongruous, but there is no question that sexuality is a form of gaining acceptance and affection. It is better to give acceptance and affection to children in as many innocent ways as possible, that they may be less inclined to seek them through relationships they are not yet prepared to enter.

I once asked a boy who was considered to be a behavior problem to return a pair of cymbals to the music room. We had used the cymbals to go out on the football field and record the speed of sound in air. No teacher in their right mind would let this kid go down the hallway with the quintessential noisemaking instrument while other teachers had class in session. Yet, it was a chance to give him the trust others had denied him, and let him have the feeling of honoring the trust of another. He showed me, and he showed himself that he is trustworthy. In seeing himself as a trustworthy and knowing that others could honor that, his maturation raced into overdrive.

An irony in the advice to praise kids regularly is the possibility of overkill. I've attended awards ceremonies, where the auditorium is left knee deep in the discarded certificates of achievement that students did not take with them (because every kid got five or more certificates). When we are seeking to pat ourselves on the back for our ability to pat kids on the back, they can sense it. Positive reinforcement should be more immediate, but less formal. If a teacher is walking down the hallway and a student stops to help another student pick up books that were dropped, it does not hurt to pass by and just say: That was very nice of you. If it is a child who typically gets in trouble, I say word for word, what I would say to a kid who never gets in trouble: That was very nice of you. A pointless and petty way to make the whole thing backfire with a difficult kid is to say: That was very nice of you… for a change. Why remind the kid that they have a reputation? Always look for that U-turn moment. It should be a given that a teacher addresses bad behaviors when they occur, so there is no need to bring them up again in a moment which could be a turning point.

New definitions of parenthood

The cause and effect relationship of parental misbehavior and student issues was unintentionally captured by the New York Post on Father's Day, 2011. The paper referred to men who have sired dozens of children via sperm banks (129 in one case, 72 in another, etc.) as "superfather's". A sperm donor does not even fit the definition of being a father. How can such a man be a "Superfather"? How can a man indifferently allow his children to be raised in completely unknown conditions, by people he never met, while he does not even know or care if these children live? Selling sperm is to be mild, an undignified way to make a living.

Juxtaposed with the article on sperm donor dads, in the same edition of the Post was an article on the changing spending habits of New York City schools. During the 1999/2000 school year, schools spent $996 per student on "Instructional Support", this covers psychologists, drug counselors, etc. By the 2008/2009 school year that figure was $1,869. When such expenses double in less than a decade, there are issues that must be studied.

In a world where too many children are unwanted, unloved and unguided by their own parents, the funding necessary to correct problems associated with bad parenting becomes overwhelming. Keep in mind that when we look at per child spending, we are not looking at a cost which is distributed to every child. Many children receive no such services.

There are seemingly endless sources of stresses for children. There are children being raised in gang cultures, being raised in poverty and being exposed to daily doses of extreme violence. There are also parents whose two incomes minimize time for building emotional ties with their children. If a couple owns a Beemer and a Benz, lives in a 10,000 square foot home and is ignoring their children to focus on two incomes, their priorities need to be adjusted.

There are parents whose chemical dependencies carry so much greater importance than their children's own lives that it has been documented where a female drug addict pimped out her two year old. How can children survive such brutality? The answer is they can not. When education diverts its scarce financial resources to cover needs which should have been met at home, the price of education skyrockets, while the quality plummets. What we can do for children of such tragic situations is to stop accepting as normal all of the dysfunction that has had such a pernicious effect, and which has pushed our boundaries of right and wrong to this precipice. Schools are chained to society. If society improves schools will improve.

Righting this listing ship can be done, and it can be done in one generation. Redirecting a child is not about chopping down trees, it is about pruning branches. Every child you meet can be a phenomenal spouse to someone in the future, a great employee, and a great parent. Not every child is going to grow up into a Hollywood heart throb. The key is to emphasize that they do not need to be a Hollywood heart throb. There is a song about being happy for the rest of your life in which one man tells another man that his wife is ugly, and the first responds: "but she sure can cook". Personally, I don't believe in "ugly" there is beauty in everything and everyone, and beauty does not need to fit someone else's preconceived notion. Secondly, the line about the woman's cooking is so funny because it hammers home the point that being in a happy relationship is not about looking at each other, but how people care about each other.

The sad thing about Hollywood heart throbs is that they are looked at as sexual objects rather than human beings. If we want children to grow up self confident: we should see them as human beings, and see the good that is in them, and help them see the good in themselves.

Hollywood does much to steer our culture, but it does not mean we cannot live lives which are contrary to that culture.

Teachers are a secondary influence, and that is how it should be, some children have good parents, some children have bad parents. Teachers can not correct a child's home life, but they can do the best job possible for the child. Teachers should always remember it is the child's future they are responsible for, not the child's parents' past.

Parenting is such an unappreciated job. We are trained to believe the greater the importance of a job, the greater the financial compensation associated with it. This is wrong. The greatest job anyone will perform is an unpaid position. There are times when I have to tell myself that sitting down and playing a game of Yahtzee with my children is truly important. It does not seem important, but it is. It may be a time when I have paper work to catch up on, or the lawn needs to be mowed, or some other task is waiting for my attention, but I have only a limited amount of time to convey unto my children the deep love I feel for them and to help them develop into a person who will be able to succeed in the world. With that line of reasoning, a game of Yahtzee all of a sudden becomes so much more than a way to pass away an hour. It becomes a way to help my children with math, help them learn to take turns, and above all, just share some smiles with them. Consider that the golden age of jigsaw puzzles was during the great depression when families wanted inexpensive, reusable entertainment. Wholesome entertainment appeals to children.

We should not move on from the simple things that bind families just because more expensive technologies exist. Watch the interactions of children playing computer games together compared to kids playing board games together. Board games save electricity, saving fossil fuels, and they bind friendships.

Healthier interpersonal relationships for children will help them develop into adults with healthier marriages. That we have (culturally) suffered through the effects of bad advice put into practice cannot be denied. We must now consider how educators can succeed in reversing the trends that have caused the suffering we see in our youth. With improved sex education, schools can become a helpful tool in serving our youth.

Consider the feelings of romantic affection a young woman of the 1970's might hope to be showered with, compared with the feelings a young woman of today may expect to be showered with. To do so, consider the feelings expressed by men about women in these contrasting sets of lyrics: one from Jim Croce, the other from Nickelback. When popular music imbeds perceptions into the minds of young men regarding what is an appropriate compliment to a young woman, is it the fault of the youth for absorbing the messages, or the fault of the adults who did not oppose that message?

JIM CROCE—1972
If I could save time in a bottle
The first thing that I'd like to do
Is to save every day 'til eternity passes away
Just to spend them with you

NICKELBACK—2003
I like your pants around your feet
And I like the dirt that's on your knees

Sex education teachers should never merely be a sounding board for current perspectives on sexuality. As sex education teachers learn to fill their arsenals with more and more facts, they will have less time to regurgitate the misleading opinions they may have unwittingly absorbed via subjective forms of teacher training and/or the media.

The Epidemiology of the Issue

There are numerous objective sources which should be utilized in researching facts. When students are presented facts, they will still have the responsibility to make the best choices in their own lives, but will be better able to make the best choices. The National Institutes of Health and Centers of Disease Control are excellent sources for objective quantitative data. Using the data available from these sources, you will see that the highest rates of STD incidence among women are found in the late teen years. That corresponds with the highest rate of STD incidence in men occurring in the early twenties. The obvious conclusion: Teenage girls are being infected by older males. This is minimized when we emphasize a man's responsibility to care about the welfare of young women on one end, and we emphasize these facts to the young ladies who are being manipulated, on the other end.

Thereby we are giving young women something to think about before entering sexual relationships.

The media will never acknowledge that they influence the behaviors of their viewers when it comes to encouraging negative behaviors, but they will charge hundreds of millions of dollars for commercial time during the Super Bowl. I don't want to focus on the buying habits of consumers exposed to car commercials during sporting events, but by sticking to the subject at hand, we can refer to an article published in the 116th issue of Pediatrics, pages 303-326. S. Liliana Escobar-Chavez found that in comparing TV exposure among adolescents, those in the 90th percentile were twice as likely to engage in sexual activity as those in the 10th percentile. The fallacy that TV does not influence the behaviors of the viewers is trumped by reality. As to the question of the prices for a Super Bowl commercial, yes those prices are legitimized, TV does influence behavior.

As teens are increasingly exposed to more and more sexuality on TV, they grow up with a new set of norms. In 1998, long after *The Waltons* and *Little House on the Prairie* had left the air; there was sexual content in 56% of TV programming. That rose to 70% by 2005, and still climbs. That leaves parents with less than 30% of programming as appropriate for children. It is important to consider that the new norms will then affect the mindset of the next generation of screen writers. Unless they choose to expose themselves to more than what is currently produced for TV, we will end up in a downward spiral. The vulgarity of a Comedy Central Roast when compared to a Dean Martin roast is alarming. The effort to be witty has been completely eradicated and replaced by a willingness to be as offensive as possible. That does not mean that wit is dead. Optimism still prevails when I see a video like "Biologist's Saint Patrick's Day Song" on You Tube. The brilliance of a young man with such a wit easily keeps hope alive.

Having mentioned *Little House on the Prairie*, we can compare how within one generation our culture shifted, leading into the 1990's. Melissa Gilbert from *Little House on the Prairie* portrayed a young lady in a family on a TV show where every episode carried a strong moral message. When her younger sister, Sara, hit the airwaves in *Rosanne*, her character was talking about being felt up as a prepubescent child. Increasingly, it seems as though there is a gauntlet which prevents a woman of morals from gaining entrance into the acting profession. Take any current actress, review her list of credentials, and try to find one who has a long list of success without one provocative/exploitative movie role on her resume.

Teresa Wright an Academy Award winner who enjoyed a 60 plus year career once refused to pose in a bikini, and argued for her right to choose modesty. She lost her contract with Samuel Goldwyn for that reason. Doing so, she gives young ladies of today a role model they can admire unflinchingly. During the 2013 Academy Awards, there was an inappropriate song illustrating the reality that current actresses cannot be modest and succeed; the way Jennifer Lawrence's face lit up when she was singled out as having not succumbed to the "success for skin" culture of Hollywood made my night. As to the song itself, it was further evidence of cultural decline.

Returning to the presentation of facts in high school and middle school sex education classes; sex-ed instructors should be able to recite data on incidence and prevalence of different STDs. It is important to differentiate between incidence and prevalence. Incidence is the occurrence of disease. Prevalence is the presence of the disease in society. Consider the incidence rate of HIV or HPV in the USA. 40,000 new cases of AIDS per year can be confirmed from nih.gov. The CDC reported in 2000 that 24% of inner city teenage girls were infected with the Human Papilloma Virus. These facts are more frightening than any statistics you may find regarding gonorrhea or syphilis. A bacterial disease can be cured with antibiotics, while viral diseases are life long trials. Sex education teachers must emphatically warn children about these statistics, tell them the only way to guarantee avoidance of these diseases is abstinence, and reassure the children that their time of celibacy will not last forever.

Does abstinence education decrease the rate of STD infections when compared to condom based sex education? No.

Why would I then even advocate for its employment? The reason is because abstinence based education causes a delay in the onset of sexual activity. If then, the delayed onset of sexual activity associated with abstinence education was coupled with the likelihood of using protection provided by the condom based form of sex education, we would then have the benefit of both. The flaw in abstinence based education is that it ignores what to do after the period of abstinence comes to an end. An educator can present proper use of contraception without advocating for a sexually active lifestyle during high school.

Saturation Levels

Within the world of education, there are many examples, and more daily, of how school environments and events further diminish our platform of authority in this realm. A disturbing example was reported in the New Jersey Star Ledger on 9/17/2004. The defendant in the sexual assault case was the school principal. What happens when the defendant has access to the files and documents of the victim? This is why the turn our nation has made on the value we assign to the character of leaders must be rectified. During the Clinton presidency, one affair after another would surface. Increasingly people would chant the mantra: It is not about his private life, it is about his job performance. We absorbed that too well. I prefer the old school line of reasoning about politicians: If his wife can't trust him, why should I? What we accept from public figures, we eventually accept from ourselves.

Is teen sexuality bad? Yes. Waiting a few years to be emotionally prepared for such a relationship is not so awful. In 2006, the cost of teen childbearing to the taxpayers was 9.1 billion according to the AP, as published on 10/24/08 in the Easton Express Times. That figure climbs. Texas itself had a bill for 1 billion dollars in 2006. We all know that even if a teen has employment it does not come with health care insurance. The article further goes on to state that "The children [of children] are more likely to be in foster care and less likely to graduate from high school. The daughters are more likely to have teen births themselves, the sons are more likely to be incarcerated." So why do we feel a need to be wishy-washy about our opposition to teen sex? Teen pregnancy is after all, the result of teen sex.

Gladly say to kids: go to movies, hold hands, get a burger afterwards; enjoy this time of life, but don't convince yourselves that it is the best time to become sexually active. End the date with a kiss and go home. There are more than enough other voices to give them the contrary message, and I only need to be accountable for the messages I give them. They should delight in the innocent infatuations they have. If I want 100% of my advice to be accepted, I can say exactly what I know people want to hear. If I want to live with myself, I need to say what I believe to be in the best interest of the young person with whom I am speaking.

Despite, numerous precise examples, the issue of teen sex is not an individual, case by case problem. It is cultural. The same way that sexually graphic and shamelessly brutal video games are a cultural problem. On 10/28/09, an assault on a 15 year old girl in California was reported that was horrific not only because the girl was savagely beaten by a gang while they raped her, but because 20 other students watched it and did nothing. We have killed the natural instinct to react instantly and forcefully to brutality. We have accustomed children to watching sexuality and violence hand in hand.

Perhaps, each of us changes as we acclimate ourselves to the climate of the culture in which we live. Like a frog in a pot of cool water, which is gradually heated until boiling, the frog does not notice the gradual changes until those changes are sufficient to kill him. I remember watching a Jodie Foster movie entitled *The Accused*, when it was in the theaters. I saw it maybe a decade later on TV or video. While watching it the second time, I did not remember seeing the rape scene. In 1988 I was a full grown man, and yet I did not look at that scene. A decade later, I was trying to understand how I was able to watch it and why I did not remember that scene when I had watched the movie earlier. I had changed; I no longer had the intrinsic gut reaction to look away from such a scene in a movie.

I speak with students who tell me that their parents would let them watch R-rated movies when they were five. Whether we are born good or bad, as a psychologist would query is no longer the question. The question is how can we return to a state of appropriate revulsion for revolting things? What our nation needs is for the next generation to be better than mine. There are more than enough good children to make that possibility a reality. The only requirement is that they understand the difference between right and wrong.

It is a rough world out there for relationships; but as Redbook Magazine pointed out on page 96 of their April 2012 edition: Just one meeting with an attorney could buy a husband and wife a weekend at a nice spa. One month's legal bills could buy them a full course of couple's therapy and countless date nights. When American adults determine to pursue healthy relationships, America's children will have more stable home lives and healthier images of what relationships can be.

CHAPTER NINE

Coaching and Extracurricular Activities

"A champion is someone who gets up when he can't."

~ Jack Dempsey

Involvement with extra-curricular activities, rounds out a young person's education. All the best reasons for advocating on behalf of extracurricular activities sound corny, but they are not. They allow students to have time with friends, have a chance to make new friends, learn teamwork, learn how to apply themselves, in the case of sports, to go outside and have a chance to run around. It gives them a chance to be the hero and be applauded by their friends. When they are the goat, they have a chance to be supported by their team mates and then try to do better next time. Via extracurricular activities, they are exposed to the arts, they are challenged academically and they are stretched as people. When they take advantage of the opportunities with which they are presented they become more well rounded, and they build happy memories with their friends.

I was a high school junior the first time my cardiologist allowed me to play competitive football. It had always been a dream of mine to play. I joined a team coached by a highly respected coach in the New Jersey Shore Conference. We were perennial contenders for the state title. A couple of the coaches made it painfully clear that they had no need for a junior with no prior experience and an abysmal level of conditioning on such a team. Being too dim to take the hint, I played for my junior and senior year, and have always been glad for that. I made some great friends whose company I still enjoy to this day, and for the first time in my life got into good shape. It never paid off in high school, and earning one varsity letter playing Division III football was hardly the apex of athletic accomplishment others have experienced, but it was still a validation that achieving goals is possible through hard work.

I did earn one enjoyable item due to athletics, a week of alternate duty in the Coast Guard playing front row for their rugby team. I loved getting away from my ship, and loved being stationed at the Presidio in San Francisco. After practice and/

or games, I could walk through a wooded lot behind the base and end up with a view of the Golden Gate Bridge. That was a seemingly small reward, but not if you knew how much I enjoyed time away from my ship.

The Greatest Gain

Ultimately, the greatest gift of participation in athletics is a good work ethic. Trying out for athletics meant I had to try to compensate for a big deficit of conditioning when compared to other life long athletes. Following my first year of college football, I had to withdraw from school due to finances. When I returned, I again gave football a shot, while commuting to save money, but again fell into financial trouble. A car that broke down twice a month was not helping, I was failing my classes and eventually, money ran out, and I again had to withdraw. Draining my bank account ended a very unpromising football career, but provided better priorities.

Replacing football was more and more work, construction when I could get it, fast food during the nights, working in a fitness center, and finally loading trucks. When I earned my degree, the work ethic I had developed specifically to play sports paid off. Only 19% of the athletes who entered my college as football players graduated. A student athlete without the financial backing to attend college, must carefully consider the trade off they are making when dedicating their time to college athletics without the benefit of a scholarship.

For a kid who was never a great athlete, and had no promise through athletics in his future, just trying hard to become an athlete created the unexpected outcome of learning to work hard. Knowing how to work hard has made a big difference in my life. It is the thing I believe to be the most important trait to share with athletes when working as a coach.

A coach should understand that the work ethic kids learn because they want to succeed in sports will later benefit them when facing the trials of life. If a child wants to play sports, a coach should encourage that, and treat them well regardless of their ability level. A less talented athlete needs to accept their place on the depth chart, but they should never in any way be mistreated due to athletic deficiencies. Sometimes, for an athlete's own welfare, they should not participate. Placing a kid with poor hand eye coordination at third base where lines drives will be shot like rockets at them is asking for trouble, but teaching a young person to maintain the stats book and letting them practice with the team builds them up, and gives them an important role on the team.

A coach may call a kid a quitter for ending his or her devotion to a sport, but will not track him or her down and try to help them reenroll if a sport leads to their dropping out of college. They will recruit a new player. A young person learning that they are expendable to a team is hard, but it is good to know. Coaches, like all people, are as individual as people in any other profession. The best coach I ever played for was a man named Coach Cleary during my freshman year in college. What made him my favorite was a simple statement: "Dan, you are messing up your plays, go talk to Bernie and ask him to explain the playbook to you". No machismo nonsense, no belittling me, he told me exactly what I was doing wrong, and how to fix it.

Our national commitment to sports can go overboard. There is nothing wrong with knowing some sports facts. I know that Graig Nettles hit 390 career homeruns, but his .248 batting average keeps him out of the Hall of Fame despite being one of history's greatest defensive third basemen. Another thing I know is that I am no football team's "12th man". No football team needs me in the stands cheering for them. They do not need my opinions about what they should have done with two minutes remaining on third down in the red zone spouted to some DJ with a radio talk show on the local sports station. The only thing they need from me is revenue so they can pay their first round draft pick. If a man is ever accused on not being a "real fan" by a true fanatic, he should take it as a compliment, then get back to taking care of his family. The American preoccupation with sports can be quite excessive. There is nothing wrong with being a sports fan, as long as priorities are not skewed.

High school coaches do well when they make every athlete work hard, stay positive, learn the game and have a chance to succeed. A fraction of one percent of high school athletes will earn a Division One scholarship. It makes no sense for a person to gear their coaching to that fraction of one percent. A coach should gear their coaching to the full 100%. There are qualities a student athlete will need to have with them after sports have ended. For most kids, organized sports will end when high school ends, perhaps after college, but even for a professional hall of famer, there is the eventual end. I can easily name 5 professional athletes who blew through over 100 million dollars, ending up bankrupt before I even search for names. Even without following such news items closely, it is possible to see how an athlete may be given every reward possible for their athleticism and without the proper footing in life, it will eventually blow up in their face. This is why work ethic and character need to be the most important traits emphasized by coaches. They benefit every child, including the future Division One star.

With our sports idol culture, it becomes more difficult to find those athletes who are wonderful to present to children as role models. Still, there are enough to make the point. Among such players during my life time, Cal Ripkin comes to mind, as does Jim Thome, Barry Sanders, Jeremy Lin and Walter Payton. These are men who display character traits that can make people successful in life regardless of where their talents lie. A coach should share the proper techniques necessary to succeed in the sport, and a coach might share with athletes stories of how Walter Payton's mom would have a truck load of dirt delivered every summer, and Walter would have to spread it around the yard. He was building strength while building a work ethic. It demonstrates how success is often the product of a good work ethic. Using sports as a way to encourage a good work ethic is commendable. Setting up athletes on pedestals is problematic.

With many of today's athletes, we are fed nonsense such as: the assault charges have been dealt with, the plea deal that allows my client to play sports while serving his one year of probation indicates that justice has been served, now let's get on with the business of playing sports. There are many names you can attach to that quote. Regardless of which name you throw in there, the message is the same: Athletes are our idols; they will do what they want. When a current day high school coach is facing such a culture, there are no rules against grabbing an old video of Roberto Clemente and showing today's generation what kind of athleticism an honorable man can exhibit.

Destroying Trust

Here is a headline from a March 2nd, 2007 copy of the Easton Express Times: "Coach pleads guilty to videotaping girls". A coach was videotaping girls in their locker room. His lawyer tried to have the tape thrown out of evidence because the girls had to commit burglary to obtain it. I applaud those girls, and I applaud the judge who refused to suppress the tape. The girls were not the police, so they are not held to the same standard when obtaining evidence, and more importantly, they stood up for themselves and each other. The coach turned out to be more than a voyeur. He had molested numerous girls on various occasions. I like the way those girls fought back against their lecherous coach. The story illustrates both what is going wrong with our society, and what type of approach is needed to correct the problems.

That story brings up another point, children should respect but not revere coaches. There is a set of behaviors which are important in society regarding the correct way to show others respect. However, putting a coach on a pedestal rather than just showing respect is setting up a situation where trouble may occur.

Should we cheer athletes regardless of circumstances? Do we cheer them because they are that much more important to the world than we are? That should not be the message we send. Coaches must be willing to correct that misperception. A high school coach needs to have their reserves prepared to take the field when they apply the correct punishment to a starter who misbehaved. It will not hurt a young man to lose a start or two. It is better for a child to be punished by an educator than be coddled by an educator and punished by a correctional officer, or a cell mate. If a student gets detention on the day of the big game, a coach should not defend the player or try to help them out of that consequence. They are better off in the long run learning accountability. Too often, young people who are not held unaccountable for a small infraction will be later found guilty of a major infraction. Let them, with kindness as the goal, learn lessons as gently as possible.

When we see abuses of all kinds at the professional level, they travel down to the high school level. On 10/22/2010, the Washington Post reported the results of a law suit where a cheerleader, having been assaulted by an athlete, was forced to cheer for her assailant or be kicked off the team. Her report of sexual assault lead to a conviction of simple assault for the athlete, thus his probation allowed him to continue as a high school athlete. She, being a cheerleader was then expected by administrators to cheer for him. I have reserved an entire section of this book to discuss the good, bad and abominable decisions of administrators.

In these cases, it can be difficult to know who to believe, the victim or the attacker. If in fact, the athlete was truly innocent of the sexual assault, and it was merely a physical assault, the outcome remains the same. He does not get cheered by that young lady because he physically assaulted her. Her right to participate in school activities out shines his right to be cheered by her. Commitment to sports must never be allowed to supersede commitment to justice,

Old School

So, if this is what sports creates in people, why even have sports in schools? Well, because there are a great many sports personalities who embody what we are trying to encourage, and because sports are good for kids. Tom Brokaw called the World War II generation our greatest generation. Is he correct? They certainly are the greatest generation with whom I have shared the earth.

Whether our founding fathers or the Civil War generation should be left out of that discussion is a debate for another time. Certainly as far as sports goes, no other generation gave us as much to be proud of outside of the arena. Gil Hodges was a Marine who fought in the Pacific. Ralph Houk was a Silver Star and Purple Heart recipient. They are representative of that generation of athletes.

When people start talking about the Yankees / Red Sox rivalry, Ted Williams will often be compared to Joe DiMaggio. To echo some of these debates, there are discussions about how much better DiMaggio was as an outfielder and base runner, and people will say that even though Ted Williams had a better batting average, he would not swing at a ball out of the strike zone even if a flare could bring in the winning run when a walk left the RBI for the next man, etc. etc. To think of Ted Williams, is to think of a man who twice left a lucrative career in professional sports to serve his country as a fighter pilot (once in WWII, and once during the Korean Conflict). This is a good thing to talk to athletes about. Encourage them not to merely be good athletes, encourage them to be great people, dependable citizens and good men or women. America can always use more good role models.

The strength an athlete builds is built for athletic competition, but should be available for situations of true importance. During one of Jerry Sandusky's sexual assaults on a child, he was interrupted by a college graduate who was a former division one athlete. That should have been the cavalry coming to the rescue. Here was a trained athlete with great physical strength interrupting a sexual assault. A vicious tackle would have ended the assault. Instead, the young man, trained to confront opponents in a game, did not confront a rapist in real life. If sports do not create men who will instantly respond to such a situation, they lose that higher level of value for which they should exist.

When men and women hesitate in doing what is necessary, we increase the need to have professional authority figures present in all aspects of our lives. When Richard Reid, the infamous shoe bomber was subdued by another passenger, we were given evidence that private citizens with a sense of duty can serve well in situations which we have been trained to believe require uniformed public servants be present.

Pat Tillman is a name we should not forget. Perhaps opinion makers want us to forget him. He died due to friendly fire, and facts were hidden from the public. His memory is not about building or diminishing support for a war. The ultimate truth of that story is that a true patriot declined a 3 million dollar professional sports contract so he could serve his country. In him, was displayed the quintessence of what we hope sports will instill in young men. For the young ladies, Kristi Yamaguchi is but one of many names we can share when we speak of the class and dignity a young female athlete may display.

Still, the most simple reason for playing sports is the joy of it. "Let's play two" as Ernie Banks would say. About Ernie Banks was said: "He never complained about his team's bad luck or bad talent, never stopped playing the game with joy, never stopped giving his all, never lost his proud demeanor, and never acted like anything but a winner. He was a symbol of the Cub fan's undiminishing resilience. If he could be happy to come to the park each afternoon, then so could we." ~ Joe Mantegna

CHAPTER TEN

Focus on the Students

"When I approach a child, he [she] inspires in me two sentiments; tenderness for what he [she] is, and respect for what he [she] may become."

~ Louis Pasteur

Some people are wary of bringing children into the world. They see the violence and injustice in this world. I am conscience of, and wary of, the dangers in the world, yet I see kids on a daily basis who restore my faith in humanity.

Schools must always exist for those children, not for the careers of the adults who work in the schools; yet if adults could not feel secure in their career choice, how could we attract the type of quality individuals who will make schools exceptional for the children? We can do both, by choosing to merely prioritize. Prioritization needs only honor this question: Is the outcome involved in an event most helpful to the future success of the student or most helpful to the credentials of the adult in question?

I've coached, and as a coach, I like the team to have a successful season. This is a perfect place for a discussion of priorities. If my team practices four hours per day, will they be superb? Yes. However, they can only do that when the amount of academics is diminished to allow such commitment. Therefore the question would be: Is it better for the students to be committed to me, as a coach, having a winning season, or better for me as an adult to be committed to the student being prepared for success in college? And that is how simple it is to set priorities. Each individual student should have the ability to make the time commitment to the activity they love by not having excessive commitments made for them from too many directions. A few hours per day of free time lets the budding artist draw, lets the athlete train and lets the bookworm read.

It would be a great thing if it was universally accepted that our goal is to focus on the students. That is the tag line teachers always spout. "It is for the students." An administrator who goofed up and now wants teachers to cover their mistake will say: "It is all about the students, let's pull together". The six figure union leader will say it is all about the students while regularly attending swank dinners and expensive events that were funded with union dollars. In reality, it is often about teachers who want 2:30 dismissals and their summers off and it is often about administrators who want the highest paying jobs education has to offer. Teachers should not be lowly paid professionals. Teachers in 10 months can honestly deserve a full year's salary. Proper compensation will help in attracting higher quality individuals into the profession. However, once in the profession, staying one or two hours late each day helping kids succeed should not be rare. Teachers staying for an hour or two tutoring kids after school, then staying to cheer on students during their sporting events, while having time to mingle with parents are all advisable practices. In correcting homework, teachers can add a few helpful comments to each paper, or just assign arbitrary grades based on formulaic observations. When teachers are really working hard, those 10 months of work will deserve 12 months of pay.

If the salary of a teacher is to be on par with the salary of other professionals, the expectations should rise. Many teachers are already at that higher level of effort, and are unfairly judged with the weaker links.

In education, it is not uncommon to have colleagues who earn the secondary income for their family. We need to stop treating teaching as the second job in a family. It should no longer be the job that allows one parent to take care of the family, while the other is the bread winner. We can however, create tiers within the profession for part-time and full-time teachers.

Good teachers want to spend all of their time helping kids, and yet there are many additional duties that go along with teaching. Increasingly, there is too much competition between time spent directly interacting with kids and time spent completing paper work. For people who find that their commitment to kids is hampered by those additional school duties because family obligations prevent them from spending a few extra hours each day completing their school work, it would be nice to open another option.

Education is a profession where part time teachers, coming in for a few periods per day could be a great asset to a district. It is however wrong to treat people who approach the job like a part time effort and people who treat it like a full time profession as equals. If that change were to occur, districts would need limits on the number of staff members who could be part timers to prevent administrators from filling a school with part time, no benefit employees. Many of our current underemployment issues are directly related to corporations preferring to hire no benefit employees through temp agencies. If schools were to have part-time positions available, they would need to be limited.

I find a typical day for me includes actively teaching and instructing the children throughout the day. During prep periods, I take the time to meet with guidance counselors or set up labs, perhaps call parents. At the 2:30 dismissal time, I will have arranged to help students who are doing poorly in class, or who are doing OK, but want to do better. It may be 4:00 by the time the last student has cleared out. At that time, I begin grading papers. When grading papers, a teacher should always try to find a few mistakes that need to be addressed, and write notes to the student regarding where improvement is needed. Once the next day is planned, it is typically 6:00 PM. If winter sports are in season, I will try to catch each team at least once per season, leaving me with a 9:00 departure time. The time necessary to do the job correctly varies significantly from the time necessary to honor one's contract. A 2:30 departure time is great for days when a person needs to make a doctor's appointment, or be home for a child's birthday, but it is insufficient time to truly be all that a student needs a teacher to be. Naturally, for a coach, all that additional grading work cannot even begin to be done until about 6 PM.

Jonathan

There are too many teachers who do not care about pursuing excellence, but care about summers off and 2:30 dismissals. This discourages the teachers who truly care. For teachers who struggle with the realities of the profession, it is good to read Jonathan Livingston Seagull.

Jonathan was a seagull who loved to fly. He tried everything he could to fly better and more skillfully. He was berated, attacked and disliked by the other seagulls. They only wanted to fly so they could find a fish to eat. To them flying was a means to an end, not a passion. If you are a person considering teaching as a career, understand that there are teachers who do not truly love teaching. It is a means to an end. However, rather than seeking a fish to eat with the littlest effort, they seek a paycheck with the littlest effort.

Here is the encouragement: despite the fact that teachers who do the minimum receive the same paycheck as teachers who give the most, the truest measure of an excellent teacher is what the students receive. The lazy seagulls of education cheat the kids in their classes. Often those kids do not realize the extent to which they were cheated. Students may have liked the lazy seagull teachers the best, and disliked the seagulls that worked hard, because the seagulls that worked hard, wanted the students to work hard. A lazy teacher is a treat to a student. No homework, low end concepts covered in class, and lots of "free time". "Free time" is the time students are given to hang around while the teacher does not ply their trade.

The Tradeoff

The benefit of working hard is never lost. In education, it merely goes to the student, rather than the teacher's salary. It is a tradeoff one has to be willing to make if they wish to be the best educator they can be. It is important to know however, that the effort was not lost. It does not show up in a teacher's paycheck, it shows up in the student's life. This is why it is important to focus on the students.

We must stop accepting the conventional wisdom about education that all teachers are equal. We need to accept that American education is regularly ranked last among industrialized nations because all teachers are not equal. Our power as a nation needs to turn away from being based on military strength and borrowing power, we need to rejuvenate our intellectual power. This begins with seeking to have the highest quality schools. That teaching was once a profession that allowed a shortened work day, with summers off as an ideally dovetailed job for people with family responsibilities needs to change. It should become a profession for people with the career ambition of creating brilliant students.

Gender issues regarding students always seem to point towards our need to improve female participation in math and the sciences. I have always had great female students. Where gender issues are most disturbing is in the number of boys who are falling into failure. They are failing in academics at higher rates, they are failing in life at higher rates, they are committing suicide at higher rates, and those suicide rates can be confirmed at cdc.gov. We see those statistics in number of discipline referrals in schools, we see those statistics in inmate populations with 9:1 male to female ratios, and we see the opposite statistics in the number of boys who take AP classes in high school and who take the highest level courses. I have so many questions and concerns about the welfare of boys, because I see their struggles year after year. This year, my freshman honors science class has 20 girls and 5 boys. The physiology class I have which is for seniors and covers college material has 22 girls and 3 boys.

A colleague once sent around one of those "feel good" e-mails. A teacher wrote a short story about a boy in her 2nd grade class who was a poor student. The little boy dressed sloppily, had bad hygiene, and performed poorly academically. As time went on, the teacher found him increasingly distasteful. She explained how it became a joy to write big fat Fs on his papers, (and most of his papers were Fs). About half way through the year, she had a conference and read through the boy's file. A year earlier, he had been a straight A student, earning praise from his 1st grade teacher. When she read further into his file she saw that his mother had died the year before. She then began to treat the boy well. He eventually came back around, and when he grew up he invited that teacher to his wedding. The moral of the story was that it was great for her to receive recognition as a wonderful teacher. I did not see her as a wonderful teacher.

Teachers should not need to know about a student's hardships as incentive to treat them well. They should never take joy writing big fat Fs on a child's paper. It is a teacher's job to find out early what is going on when a child is struggling. If a child comes to class everyday in an unkempt and unwashed manner, a teacher should try to help that child. As a second grader, the boy was 7 years old. How can a person take joy in the failure of a 7 year old? For me, the moral of that story is not based on the happy ending, but all of the wrong behaviors exhibited by the teacher initially.

In dealing with students, a teacher should err on the side of compassion.

The Trouble with Boys

Regarding discipline, I do not see the outrageous inequality among the genders in my class that I see in other classes. My boys rarely get detention, and they rarely misbehave. I do not ignore misbehavior, but I address it without trying to humiliate or belittle the boy as a way of showing my power and control of the class. I give them a detention, appeal to their sense of reason, and let them go shortly thereafter provided they promise to cut out the nonsense. They promise to try harder, and they do. Concomitantly, the female students I have smash through the stereotypes about females and science. They are brilliant. Still, females are outpacing boys in all possible positive markers, and the boys are falling behind. Our boys need our help.

My background as a sailor, construction worker, and dock worker makes connecting with boys easier. Such a background is atypical in a classroom. When men get into the workforce, there is a type of man who goes into construction, becomes a fireman, a policeman or a mechanic, etc. These men, being employed elsewhere, are naturally, underrepresented in teaching staffs of schools. In the first place, only 7% of elementary school teachers are male, and there are only about 35% of high school teachers who are male. We are grossly outnumbered, and we fall within the boundaries of being men who like academics.

Who then should these future construction workers, firemen and mechanics bond with? Well, each other and hopefully some good teachers. As is chronicled in Peg Tyre's book *"The Trouble with Boys"* there are boys who just do not fit into the traditional pattern a teacher wants. They are boys who want to be in the sandbox playing with a toy bulldozer, or pointlessly tackling each other. They will soon find themselves regularly getting into trouble, and falling behind in academics. There is nothing wrong with a having a soft spot for these boys. When I take out a group of students for an outside activity, I know which boys will immediately tackle each other. As long as no one was involved who did not want to be involved, I tell them to knock it off and rejoin the group. They knock it off and rejoin the group.

They were not going to act like that all period. They just had to get it out of their system. Not everyone has a comfort zone with a little bit of silly behavior, if the behavior is a rarity, it is best to address it without making it a capital crime.

One certainty is that humor is often a better behavior adjustment than discipline. Suppose a student puts his or her head down on the desk, some teachers will ask that student a question they will not know the answer to, as a means of embarrassing the kid. A trip to the office is an option. Some teachers like to drop something heavy and loud next to the student. Others are happy to leave well enough alone, and just be happy the kid is not annoying classmates. To me, it is a great chance to get the kid's head back in the game and give his classmates a break from the lecture. Here is a recommended response: "Hey Billy, you awake? Did you hear about the ship's captain during the Napoleonic wars? Well, his lookout reported two enemy ships on the horizon. Immediately, the ship's captain commanded his ensign to retrieve his red shirt from the cabin below. The captain puts on the shirt, and led his men to victory over the two ships in a brilliant battle. Later, the ensign asks: Why did you need the red shirt? The captain responds that he must look brave, and never let his crew know if something happened that would cause them to feel fear. With a red shirt, even if I was shot, they would never know I was bleeding, so they would never lose heart. The ensign applauded his bravery and strategy. A few days later, the look out reported that there were ten enemy ships on the horizon. The captain looked at the ensign and said: Go below, and bring me my brown pants.

The two minutes that story cost me, could have also been spent arguing with the sleepy head. As it is, the sleepy head is now awake, and the rest of the class enjoyed the diversion. When teaching for 42 minutes or more per period, a teacher will inevitably lose a couple of minutes here or there. It is better to make it fun than miserable for the kids.

So we see that we are at a juncture where a commitment to students, needs our utmost attention. The kids are, and naturally should be, the primary focus. Should that mean that teachers should not support each other?

Child versus Coworker

Teachers often support each other, and they should. The idea of having a union is meaningless if the only thing wanted of us is the $1,100 per year taken from our salaries as dues. Supporting fellow teachers is appropriate unless a teacher is faced with the decision of supporting the best interests of a student or the rights of a teacher who failed in their duty to the child. As far as the union goes, it often seems the $1,100/year shakedown is of greater importance to them than teachers supporting each other.

Teachers should be opposed if they are preventing proper education from occurring through their actions. Opposition is also important if something is going on where the welfare of the children is at stake. Should a fellow teacher ever commit an act that needs to be reported, my personal belief is that the report must be made. However, it is also important to speak directly to the other teacher, let them know what you felt needed to be reported so as to accept responsibility for your own actions and also to let the other teacher know that representation may be necessary; in that way, should the report be false, the other teacher will not be blindsided by an overzealous administrator.

Direct and honorable behavior is not always the plan of the day in education. I've worked with great administrators who exert every possible effort for kids. Then, there are times in watching the actions of some administrators (some of whom were subpar teachers of average intelligence) when it seems they are specifically taught how to be duplicitous and devious in the way they handle situations. There are times when doing what is in the best interest of students means a teacher is not doing what is in the best interest of his or her career.

One of my experiences when dealing with the best interests of children over the best interest of my career came when my school experienced a gas leak.

During the gas leak, the custodian who discovered the leak made a report and sought to have the children evacuated. The head maintenance man in any district has a black seal and is certified on how to handle any crisis with the boilers. People need to listen to him when he speaks on such issues. As he explained it, after much arguing, the principal finally agreed to evacuate the children. However, rather than simply make a standard evacuation announcement, the message was spread by word of mouth. I was in the hallway at that time, and was approached by a secretary with the news. I then raced around my side of the building to evacuate everyone. After going back to the office to alert them that my side of the building was empty, I left with the remaining staff members.

While exiting, it occurred to me that I really did not personally know about the other side of the building. I went back in, did another run through in the opposite wing of the building, and found a group of special education students with their teacher. They were in a small room at the end of the hallway and were passed over. After evacuating them, I reported the series of events to the superintendent.

It happened that the failed evacuation had been hidden from the board, and the principal was being praised for an amazing job of evacuating kids. Following up with a truthful report to the board resulted in fallout from this event. Teacher concern for students is not always appreciated. The students' best interests should always be first and foremost. That is not always the case, as schools sit at the intersection of adults' careers and the students' welfare.

This is important for future teachers to understand: "Play the game" and "Cover your tracks" are the watch words in education. That is a travesty. The watchwords should be: "Do what is right for the kids at all times, and keep yourself employable outside of education".

I once worked in a district where the man who was the best teacher died of a heart attack at 56. He always put out the extra effort and always volunteered for activities to benefit the kids. His loss was tragic, other losses to the district were avoidable. With increased issues arising due to administrative failings, soon many additional teachers were leaving to take work elsewhere. It was sad to see the train of good teachers leaving that school during the time of one superintendant, knowing that the kids could never understand what was happening behind the scenes. The kids only knew that they were constantly losing one excellent teacher after another.

Icebergs and Styrofoam

When I think of that excellent teacher who died young while exerting every effort possible to benefit kids, I think of an iceberg. 10% is visible, 90% is hidden below the surface. He was an iceberg. Great teachers are icebergs. They are working tirelessly, but are not seeking attention for their efforts. Great administrators need to understand that the teachers who photograph every activity their students have ever done are blocks of Styrofoam. 100% of their substance floats on the surface. Styrofoam does not need to be praised, icebergs need to be appreciated.

Objective Measures of Success

Such a crisis situation as the gas leak is a rarity. In my 18 years in the classroom, the gas leak was the only time it was actually necessary to evacuate kids. Schools do fire drills twice each month, but schools never burn down. They are made of cinder blocks. Still, we do fire drills just to make sure the students know what to do when an emergency occurs. As far as day to day knowledge goes, we also need to insure they have learned the material for which they are responsible. If they know what to do should a fire occur in a cinder block building, they should know what to do when they are solving a math problem. This is where standardized testing rears its head. Standardized testing allows a community to know if the children are actually learning. Grades can be deceiving. An "A" from one teacher may mean the student showed up and did not disrupt class, while with another teacher, it may mean the student is ready for college.

Standardized testing is such a troublesome issue. It is very expensive, and it is contentious. However, it is necessary. The problem is that students do not have the experience to realize what type of education they are receiving. A chef may look over a cut of meat and decide to send it back to the butcher, because a chef has seen millions of cuts of beef and knows quality. A student just accepts the education they are provided without questions. A chef can identify a rancid slab of meat from a top cut. A student has no idea what they are receiving, they've never received an education before.

A good friend of mine was once fired from his position despite being an excellent teacher. Being an excellent teacher does not always mean much in education. Some administrators like excellent teachers, some prefer malleable mediocrity, some like eye candy, and some like to be surrounded by old friends being issued tax money as if it were coming from the administrator's own personal piggy bank.

When that excellent teacher was replaced by an inexperienced teacher, the difference was remarkable. What was visible during the transition time through a teacher's eyes would not have been discernable to a layperson walking through the school building. To a lay person, the two teachers would have seemed to be equivalent. However, under my friend's guidance, the students while studying the Revolutionary War could name all the major battles, and the changing strategies of England and they could also explain how the writings of Hobbes, Voltaire and Locke influenced the thoughts of the founding fathers. Any person having a discussion with these students, would be amazed at what they knew.

When we took a trip to Independence Hall in Philadelphia, our group of kids answered every question asked by the tour guide. They had a pride in their knowledge that shone forth with the kind of joy kids normally emote after a great play in an athletic competition. After that man was fired, he was replaced by an inexperienced teacher who was well liked by the kids and well trained in pedagogy, but did not have the same knowledge base or experience as the teacher who had been lost. The focus during the Revolutionary War unit changed. The students no longer were learning all of the names, dates and ideas of the era. They spent two weeks creating their own Constitution. Now to an outside observer, both classes were running smoothly. Both groups of kids were engaged and well behaved. The difference lies in what they came away with. The second group relived the Constitutional Convention while creating a Constitution for the school. However, they debated over whether or not students could chew gum in school or wear hats on Fridays. The first group completed the unit full of knowledge. The second group did not. There is a great difference between keeping kids occupied and educating kids. We must avoid activities that seek merely to keep kids occupied. Teachers must advocate for activities that fill kids' heads with knowledge.

If students are given a series of hoops to jump though as a means to an end, they can very well end up knowing little, despite having jumped through all of the hoops they were directed through. Standardized testing is a proper way to assess if any knowledge has been absorbed. Does using standardized testing favor some students over other students? Yes, but that is the point. Well prepared students will be more successful.

Any teacher will be proud when their students do well on a standardized test, as it validates what the teacher has done in the classroom. It is wrong to "teach to the test", but if the students have been equipped with enough general knowledge on the subject, and coached in how to focus and concentrate while testing, they will do well. When funds for standardized testing were too low to do more than the basics, standardized tests were limited to math and English. For a science guy, there were naturally some tears of sadness for having been left out. Not the big gushing, heaving, sobbing tears of sadness that occur when someone eats the last slice of pizza, just the small trickling tear of feeling left out. That being said, a student who does well in English can read. A student who does well in math can add. With a functional capacity in those two disciplines, the student can also pick up a book and learn science. Studies have shown that just math and history can serve as indicators of future success. "Student grades in high school Algebra I and world history were the strongest statistically significant indicators that a student will maintain a 2.5 college GPA during the first year of college."(Davis, 2010)

Now, we enter another realm of concern from the teachers' point of view. If salaries and ratings of teachers are going to be tied to how well students perform on standardized tests, it becomes unfair, as not every teacher teaches a subject which is assessed using standardized testing. Year after year, the English teacher will need to worry about their job status, while the art teacher will not be put under the same amount of pressure.

The best example of standardized testing I've heard of is practiced by a local bar owner. When a bartender comes in asking for a job, he tells them that a customer just came in and gave a 10 dollar bill for a $6.25 tab and asks what the change will be. He eliminates 90% of the candidates in that way. That is the simplest reality of standardized testing. It is designed to test preparedness for college, but in the long run, it judges preparedness for employment.

Suppose someone wants to pursue a career as a carpenter. They will need to know some trigonometry when calculating the pitch of a roof, and have proficiency with various calculations. However, who cares if they use a comma when a semicolon is appropriate? It is more important that they be able to cut precisely, measure accurately, and assemble properly. An "end of course" project for a future carpenter may be that they be given a set amount of wood, a schematic diagram, and be directed to assemble a cantilever bridge from the pieces capable of supporting a set amount of weight. Thus, when a student graduates high school, their diploma is not one generic piece of paper, but instead is varied to indicate where they are going to head in life. A student who is not the most academic student and would graduate in the middle of their class based on academic criteria, may be the most skilled metal worker in the building and can graduate at the head of the class with a specialized industrial arts degree. Should that student at a later point in their life, wish to return to their education with a focus on specific academic subjects, they will be no more than a short drive to the nearest community college. Deficiencies in one area of an education can be addressed later in life. The rapidly changing economy of our country requires that people become lifelong learners.

Despite this advocated diversification of diploma requirements, there is still someone who is going to end up at the end of the class. Well, there certainly are enough "end of the class rank" graduation success stories that we do not need to leave those kids feeling like failures. A teacher should always encourage a student that their future is in their hands and is still being shaped. Hideki Matsui, who earned fame as a Yomiuri Giant and a New York Yankee, has stated that the greatest skill a person can have is the ability to make oneself work hard. A person can graduate at the end of their class and discipline themselves to work hard. While George Armstrong Custer is best remembered for Custer's last stand, which reminds us of the horrible part of our history known as "The Indian Wars", he was a hero at Gettysburg, and throughout the Civil War. Our part in "The Indian Wars" is a great stain on our history and the vestiges are a reminder that we still need to make amends for what has been done. However, the Civil War was a time in our history when the best we could muster in battlefield courage was on display on both sides of the field. When George Armstrong Custer prevented Jeb Stuart from reaching the battlefield at Gettysburg, the victory that changed the tide of the war was secured. George Armstrong Custer graduated at the end of his class from West Point. Those "end of the class" kids need to know that tomorrow is yet to be, and it is full of potential. However, they will need to find what it is they are passionate about and put their whole effort into it.

Kids can achieve great things, we need to trust them and help them. In the April, 2013 issue of National Geographic, pilot Barrington Irving explained that the students in the school he runs responded to a challenge. If they would build him an airplane from scratch, he would fly it. They built it, he flew it (and survived).

CHAPTER ELEVEN

Working with Parents

"Parents have become so convinced that educators know what is best for their children that they forget that they themselves are really the experts."
~ Marian Wright Edelman

There should be one common denominator between teachers and parents: the best interests of the children. In an ideal world, that comment would end this chapter. In education, there will be 100 times more positive experiences with parents than negative ones. However, those negative ones can come to dominate weeks of a teacher's life, and leave us wanting to go find any job besides education. An educator I enjoyed working with, and enjoyed gleaning wisdom from is named Anita. She had a saying: "Plant corn, you get corn". Coming from her mouth, it immediately took the edge off whatever headache you were dealing with, and provided a much needed humorous respite; it put all things in perspective. A kid who constantly and deliberately misbehaves, most likely learned to do so from his or her parent(s). In such cases, I believe in the pruning approach. You want to prune off the bad behavior, but save the good in the kid. It is wrong to punish a kid for the parent's behavior, and if anything, it is good to err on the side of being too tolerant with a student when knowing where the behavior came from. We are all human, and it is important to proactively address one's own human nature. There are two good reasons why a teacher must guard their response to such situations. One is to ease the kid out of their conditioning, and one is to make sure to not take out on a child, frustration with their parent.

My good friend Pete, who is a correctional officer, will tease me when I talk about a problem child. "Let him go, don't correct him, that is my job security" he will chide me, as if wanting a new generation of inmates. That is his sense of humor. Of course, in serious moments, he will lament the increasingly youthful population he deals with and the extent of their criminal histories. I take these conversations to heart, and honestly believe that every time I set rigid guidelines for students that I am steering them away from harsher punishments in the "real world". For all intents and purposes, a detention is barely a punishment. The student sits down for an hour and completes their homework. If a few detentions deters a child from ingraining antisocial behaviors which will manifest themselves in more violent or pernicious ways later, by all means a teacher should give as many detentions as is necessary. Office (administrative) detentions are less effective than teacher detentions. When giving a child a personal detention in my room, the duration of the detention can be greatly diminished, and a talk can be had with the student. It is better to talk with the student, explain the concerns, explain how the other student, students or adults were impacted by the situation, then ask what caused the situation. When everything is squared away, I will explain why education is so important, why I work so hard at it and why I want all of my students (transgressor included) to do well and feel safe in my classroom. The approach has not yielded 100% success, however, 99% may be a fair estimate. When a person knows they are cared about, and knows that a teacher cannot tolerate their abuse of others because the teacher cares equally about all of the students in his or her classroom, a tone is set which will create an ideal classroom environment. In those cases, where firm guidelines and respect fail, it is time to move on to administrative procedures, and if those do not work, unfortunately, it is time for Pete.

The cost of unsuccessful discipline is a burden to the whole of society. Sources vary greatly in price per year to house an inmate. If we go with the number $45,000 per year, which is common in the data I have reviewed, a rapist sentenced to a ten year stint will cost the taxpayers close to half a million dollars, probably far more once the legal proceedings are considered. This is compounded with the loss to our nation of a similar value in GDP if the inmate was being a productive member of society. To that we can add all the expenses accrued by private citizens taking precautions and purchasing items to help them be safe from criminals. Every consumer item we buy has a 15% increase in cost to offset the effects of shoplifting and to combat shoplifting via security measures. Economists seem to think that consumers have to be spending money in a nonstop fashion to keep the economy moving and to keep people employed. That is false. If we would stop generating so much need to spend money, we could live happily with less money, and spend more minutes of our lives in enjoyable diversions. This is not to belittle hard work. As a father of three, I do not lament a need to keep two jobs. It is just also important to look at the minutes of our lives as another form of currency, and I would rather spend more of that currency on my children.

The world would be better, if every parent took great pride in their children for whatever good qualities the child displayed. It is common to see bumper stickers with the message: "Proud parent of an honor student". It is harder to find bumper stickers reading: "Proud parent of an incarcerated felon". We should be proud of our children for the little things as well, helping around the house, being kind to siblings, etc. A need to praise everything is a bit of overkill, but a society with our rate of incarcerated felons is also inexcusable. In working through this discourse, it is not an intention to blow problems out of proportion. There are daily affirmations of what is good with humanity in this country; tragically, there are also almost daily news stories about gang rapes and violent fights which are videotaped and posted on social media sites. The pendulum has swung far enough. There are only so many things parents can do if we as a whole allow the disintegration of our culture. There are teachers who love to use vulgar humor with kids or who love to speak in a cavalier fashion about drug abuse. Parents have a valid reason to expect character from teachers, and should not be shy about demanding it when it is absent.

While teachers can positively affect the lives of children, some children will need more support than others.

When the news reported that a man with 30 children is seeking state help for his child support, the issue of societal responsibility came to the forefront. How sad for those children, hopefully they all somehow manage to succeed in life, but their father has put all 30 children in a situation where every aspect of their futures is in danger. Society cannot absorb all the responsibility for such parental indifference. Women should take enough time to learn about a man before having a child with him to know that he has already had two dozen children with 8 different women. The rest of us can try our best to offset whatever trials those children will endure, but an outsider is more limited than a parent.

Educators should look at every child with the understanding that perhaps the child has no structure, love or kindness at home. The slow to anger mind set will not efface the ability to discipline a student effectively, but it will affect the state of mind with which discipline is administered. I have always found that taking a child aside, and explaining to them what the problem is, helps to defuse the situation, and it helps to avoid future run-ins with the same type of situation. This is not to say that the world is full of bad parents. But they are out there, and until a teacher know a child's story, it is better to take a gentle and patient approach with them rather than coming down like a ton of bricks on a kid who may already be dealing with too many trials for their age as it is.

There are times when a student who does not respect teachers has a parent who does not respect teachers. It may be that such a parent came to that conclusion with a legitimate grudge against teachers.

Having had difficulty at one time with a student, it later came to light that his mother was a lawyer, and once during a presentation to our school she shared that as a student, her teacher told her that her choices in life were very limited. At that moment, the student and his difficult mother were no longer mysteries. Here was a woman with the ability to graduate from law school, upset at having been told by a teacher that her options were limited. That is a legitimate grudge. The next time a conference became necessary, I confided to the mother that I also had teachers who diminished my abilities the way her teacher had diminished her abilities. I assured her that I was not doing that to her son, and in fact had a sincere desire to see him succeed. That conversation was the last time I talked to that mother about discipline. All of our future conversations had to do with the success her son was enjoying in my class. Reassurance of what parents need to hear should not be too much to ask of a teacher. Living up to the expectations parents hope for, is part of a teacher's job.

CHAPTER TWELVE

Working with Administrators

True leadership must be for the benefit of the followers, not the enrichment of the leaders.
~ Robert Townsend

Daniel Helm

If you want to work in a school where the administration controls the quality of the school, think of them as the government of the school and consider a quote from Margaret Meade: "Never count on government to change anything. All significant change comes from the passion of individuals". Without passionate teachers in a school district, the administrators can do nothing.

A poor administrator wonders which teachers are best manipulated with a whip, and which are best manipulated with a carrot and stick. A great administrator fills the school with teachers who understand the importance of the profession and who seek from an administrator, only the freedom to be excellent. The lowest form of administrator will seek to be surrounded by the lowest quality teachers so as to be a gleaming gem in a sea of mediocrity.

Administrators are in a tough spot. They are caught in the crosshairs of teachers and the unions, and the parents who may or may not have reasonable or even sane demands, board members who may not always have the right reasons for being on the board, and most importantly, the best interests of the students.

In the last century, the number of lawyers per capita in this country has increased 10 fold. Lawyers solve too many problems that people should be able to solve on their own. All of these people are factors that influence an administrator's actions. To do what is right, the administrator should focus solely on the best interests of the students. However, again, it must be understood that schools are founded at the intersection of adults' careers and students' best interests. If a school is run by unethical administrators or unethical union leaders, and staying in their good graces, or getting in their good graces, is predicated on playing your role when appropriate to help them cover their own malfeasance, it is the rare person who will endanger their own career by doing what is right when they can do what is wrong, and write it off as "just doing my job, just following orders".

If we expect teachers to care more about the education they provide than the retention of their employment, we must have administrators who care more about the educational process than they care about their careers. Once all persons are on the same page with that goal, there can be a more uniform application of programs that benefit students. In fact, if everyone was only in the school to do the best job they can for the kids in that school there would be no need for any form of emotional trepidation about joining the profession.

The problem with administrators is that their salaries are too often the reason they take the step into administration. For administrators to be credible advocates of excellence in the classroom, they need to have once distributed excellence to their students. Administrators also need to be intelligent enough to see through many of the games that go on in schools.

Some degree of weeding out of poor administrators could occur through the use of GRE scores when admitting candidates to administration programs. Many administration programs do not require candidates to have taken the GRE. The GRE is basically the SAT for graduate school, just at a higher level. If we allow less than superior intellects to enter administration, and then give them the choice of being surrounded by excellence or malleable mediocrity they will choose the latter.

A great administrator I worked for in my first teaching job ran the school effectively, solved problems by being proactive and direct. When problems appeared, they disappeared almost as quickly. She hired positive people, and helped them achieve success by making her expectations clear and presenting directions not from the perspective of having power, but from the perspective of leading teachers into the correct direction to properly educate children. The notion of power in schools seems counterintuitive.

Schools should not be places of power, but responsibility. Power can deviate into the ability to do what is wrong and get away with it. Responsibility is accepting the task of doing what is right even when it is very difficult.

I have worked in all types of environments, with great administrators, good administrators, adequate administrators, inept administrators and evil administrators. Most likely, if you are thinking about becoming a teacher, you will end up somewhere in the middle. If a young teacher has the ability to choose where he or she would like to work, my advice is to find a school with stability in the administrative staff. Avoid administrators who have put in the minimum time in the classroom to qualify for an administrative position. A truly great administrator is so focused on the kids that great teachers naturally follow their lead only because they were going in that direction anyway.

Subordination to the noblest tenets of education should always be the standard by which teachers are judged. As a teacher, when my administrator is not dedicated to the best interests of the students, but subordinates the children's welfare for their own career's welfare, I have the choice of being subordinate to the kids' welfare or the administrator's ambitions. In such a case, being subordinate to the kids' best interest can be deemed insubordination to the administrator. It is still the right thing to do.

What's Out There

The Easton Express Times in a front page article on January 9, 2009 gave account of a superintendent for a New Jersey School District who was found guilty of stealing $90,000 by skimming off the cafeteria's lunch money, among others tactics employed to swindle the school district. As a result, his $142,000 salary disappeared, and he was facing 10 years in prison and the loss of his pension. That is a case where a district employee who knew about the scam, faces a choice of risking their career by reporting what they know and facing the ire of the superintendent, or keeping quiet and remaining subordinate. In that case, the good guys won, but on a daily basis, there are cases where smaller incidents go unreported or are hard to prove.

There was a case in 2007 in Bethlehem Pennsylvania, where a principal had become addicted to drugs. His teachers, through their union, had made complaints about his attendance. The attendance was only the most minimal issue at hand. His attendance issues led to closer performance evaluations, leading to a cascade of events ending with him being arrested in his office at the school watching pornography naked with a bag of crystal methamphetamine. How is that for a visual of school leadership?

Having higher expectations of professionals in education is reasonable. Whether or not that man knew the extent to which his life was spiraling out of control as he lost himself in drug dependency is beyond the scope of the article. However, long before that day he should have gotten out of education. It would be good to have more escape routes from education into private industry. Teachers and other school professionals who know they are no longer passionate about their profession often feel trapped by their pensions, health care or salaries. In the private sector, people can change jobs when opportunities arise. Teachers for the most part stay in one school decade after decade, same staff, same classroom, and same environment. If it is a good environment, that is great; if it is a bad environment, the same nonsense occurs endlessly. Some people like the comfort of that life, for others change is enjoyable.

I have always found change to be a good thing. Despite not liking the dichotomy of the Coast Guard in that officers and enlisted people were treated significantly different, there were certain aspects of the service that were very good. In the Coast

Guard, every promotion brings people into a new duty station. Even people who are not on the promotion list can switch duty stations every couple of years. A new environment can be very refreshing. Teachers are frightened to do this. Once a teacher's salary has advanced beyond a certain point, their experience becomes a liability. In the military, a twenty year veteran will hold a higher rank than a 19 or 20 year old. In the teaching profession a 22 year old novice fresh out of college is a teacher, and a 50 year old with 25 years in the classroom is a teacher. There is no distinction, so why wouldn't a business administrator pick the cheaper product? There would need to be concrete evidence that the more experienced teacher provides a better quality education than the less expensive option. That can be difficult to demonstrate. There is however, a vast chasm between the education a quality teacher provides and the education an also ran provides. That vast chasm is hard to quantify, a $20,000 savings in salary is quantifiable. One possible, inexpensive, mechanism to assess teacher ability would be to request that graduates of a high school provide feedback as to which teachers actually gave them the ability to succeed in college, and which teachers did not. By the time a young adult is 19, 20 or 21, their view on their high school education will have matured into a more objective state, and can more often than not be trusted to assess which teachers gave them the ability to succeed in life.

Assessments

Assessing administrators carries a different weight. Teachers do not graduate and move on. They remain in the school and their careers are impacted by the administrators' inclinations. In studying the leadership issues of Enron during its collapse, we can see how a corporate culture can twist into a situation where people are doing things that are unethical with the complicit cooperation of the corporation. In such a situation, doing what is right makes a person an outsider.

Proper leadership leaves those in a subordinate position happy to follow the lead of others. Poor leadership makes people want to change their station in life. As previously mentioned, questionnaires sent to graduates of a high school who are currently college students would be a good means of assessing teacher efficacy. Likewise, in that more people leave teaching than any other profession early in their careers, it would be good for the state department of education to survey teachers who leave the profession or who even leave a district as to what motivated the change.

Such surveys would allow unfettered honesty about administrator performance as they would be provided by teachers who no longer have anything to lose. At their best, administrators are great leaders, who intuitively know how to best address issues. That does not mean that all administrators are great leaders, some learned how to make decisions with an air of authority, yet without insight.

Sometimes, administrators are salesmen, maybe they do not truly understand the intricacies of their product, but they know how to say what people want to hear.

Harmonious companies do what administrators cannot. They simply fire the people who fail to perform. Tenure causes a great many problems, despite solving some other problems. Keep in mind that those harmonious companies are motivated to make a profit, and therefore they will not fire the best and the brightest. Schools can not make a profit, they can not show a loss, they just need to be. For that reason, some people believe that any teacher is expendable, provided someone else with the correct certificate can be hired to take attendance.

In addition to proper staffing of a school, administrators also need to resolve conflicts. When administrators try to find the middle ground in a conflict, each side gives up 50% of their claim on the issue. What if one person is 100% right and the other person is 100% wrong? Then the 50% rule leaves a new standard which is 50% wrong. Taken incrementally, this type of policy eventually leaves no one true standard of expectations.

The quip: "Well, we'll just agree to disagree" is a quick way to end any discussion, but what if the disagreement should be followed through to resolution? If one person says: 2+2=4, and another person says 2+2=5, you can bet it will be the 2+2=5 person saying "We'll just have to agree to disagree". Rather than agree that 2+2=4.5 as a means of making everyone happy a leader should do the math, and let the 2+2=5 person accept that they were wrong.

In education, there should be deep discussion and analysis of an issue until the truth is unearthed. Since we are discussing education, we never need to settle on a less than ideal standard. In research, the scientific method should be employed until resolution is reached. In other areas that are more subjective, we still need a standard. What is a good standard to pursue in a school? Nelson Mandela (quoted on pg 81 of the June, 2010 issue of National Geographic) said it well when he discussed the fall of apartheid and what success meant: "It will be measured by the happiness and welfare of the children". Educators have an ultimate goal: the happiness and the welfare of the students. Mr. Mandela's words are the best standard I can think of as a measure of what is the best way to find resolution when there is conflict in education.

In the April 9th, 2011 edition of the Philadelphia Inquirer, the headline read: "City may put armed police in schools". Within the content of the article was the following passage:

> "The series detailed brutal attacks on students and teachers—thousands of assaults are recorded annually"

One of the realities in such situations, when the number and severity of issues being reported are so extreme, is that we can assume that not all incidents are being reported. There is a secondary reality when such chaos reigns, huge numbers of transgressions which destroy the educational environment are being completely ignored, or accepted as within the range of expected behaviors. There is a distinction between saying "something is wrong but I can not fix it", and saying that "something is tolerable". Every time the line of what is tolerable moves farther in the direction of what is really wrong, we all lose.

The number of discipline reports in schools today is the same as it was in the 1950s. That statement is from an article which went on to explain that while the number of infractions being reported is the same, the difference is the type of incident being dealt with as a discipline issue. In the 1950s, a student chewing gum, or walking on the left side of the hallway would be sent to the principal, whereas today, there are schools where rape of students and assault of teachers have become the types of incidents that are discipline problems. Expulsion is the answer to these problems, with the problem then being turned over to the authorities.

While teachers should be patient with students, once a problem becomes an administrative issue, there needs to be stricter consequences, and if expelling a few students allows every other student to get the education they deserve, it is a decision which needs to be made. This brings us to another reason the government should endeavor to create an economy where there are more jobs which do not require college. A young person who refuses to participate in the educational process needs to have work available rather than be left in a situation where there are no hopes for employment at all. Even among college educated adults, work is becoming more difficult to find. Many of those college educated adults borrowed money at high interest rates in order to get that degree. Overwhelming student loan debt in a nation drowning in national debt, leaves us with the question: What will happened when it is time to pay the bills?

The notion of an administrator being the one who ultimately must sign off on a student's expulsion, or sign off on a student's paper work when they drop out, leads us to the question: At what age can a student accept the responsibility of an adult? Eighteen has been the standard for a long time; increasingly even older people struggle to get by on their own. Once a young person is out of the system, it is good that we have options to get back on track, whether through a G.E.D. followed by career training or via the military. As hard as teachers may work to give a child a bright future, eventually, the child must determine his or her own fate.

In that there are good administrators out there, it would be better if the bad ones were more frequently caught with their hand irrefutably in the cookie jar. Catching them with their hand in the cookie jar is much more difficult than it might seem. The reason that it is difficult is due to the social dynamics of a school. Typically for the teachers to deal effectively with a low quality administrator, a vote of no confidence is needed.

Generating a vote of no confidence is difficult. No matter how bad an administrator is, they will always have supporters, after all, they are the ones who hire employees. If a person is receiving somewhere between $50,000 - $100, 000 per year due to an administrator's decision to hire them, that employee may have a tough time placing the best interests of the kids ahead of fealty to the administrator. This is particularly true when the employee was less qualified than other candidates, but was hired due to a personal relationship with the administrator.

Administrators control a large portion of any town's tax revenue, and it is possible that they will spend that tax revenue not to improve the school, but to take over the school and make it a place where their career can survive.

There are many examples from first hand experience I could share about what goes on in schools that the general public does not know. Things I've seen have bothered me enough to write this book. My task has been trying to stay true to the book's goal, which is sharing enough truth about what goes on behind the scenes to bring awareness, while not dwelling on problems without presenting solutions. There are also many stories regarding what is right and good in education that need to be shared as education is a much maligned profession. In judging education, we can think about something Mark Twain said: "The cat, having sat upon a hot stove lid, will not sit upon a hot stove lid again. But he won't sit upon a cold stove lid, either." The problems in education are there, but so are the victories, not everything is a negative.

Success Stories

One of my favorite success stories based on an administrator's influence in a school district comes from Bergenfield School District in New Jersey. Facing a high dropout rate, the superintendent implemented a multi layered approach to dropping out where students needed to go through a sign-out procedure which involved getting teachers to sign their form, the vice principal, the principal and the superintendent. By the time a student reached the superintendent, they had been so thoroughly exposed to the truth that all of their teachers wanted them to stay that the dropout rate reached zero within a few years.

Another school which has introduced exciting innovations into secondary education is the Pathways in Technology Early College High School in New York City. "P-Tech" has associated itself with IBM, and two colleges, whereby students can complete an associate's degree while completing their high school studies. There are often fluff courses added into a student's school day. Often kids need that time to wind down, and catch their breath.

There is nothing wrong with an occasional break, but for students who feel comfortable adding in more academic courses during their day, an opportunity to take college credits during the school day is both economical and challenging.

New York City's East Side Community High School provides links to research papers published by staff members. As Doctor Benjamin Carson points out with his Scholar's Fund, it is time to celebrate student's academic achievements as much as we celebrate student's athletic achievements. Likewise, East Side Community High School is celebrating the teachers who step up the academic environment of a school, when typically, any time an educator is in the newspaper, it will be one of the coaches for a sports program.

Administrators need to honor academics; the local paper will honor the sports programs. The truth about education is that a teacher who knows how to learn is always going to be a better teacher than a teacher who has been taught how to teach. As long as administrators put those teachers in the best position to teach, they have been successful administrators.

CHAPTER THIRTEEN
Education, Politics and Unions

"Teacher unions are an interest group that acts in defense of their own interests, which means the union bosses' interests, not the members."
~ Peter Brimelow

Without unions, people stand on their own. Good teachers may do better without being linked to lower quality teachers. Many teachers are grossly overpaid, many teachers are underpaid. Teachers are all paid a standard wage regardless of the skill set they bring into the classroom, regardless of whether they work the precise 7 hours the contract demands or if they put in 10 and 12 hour days. They are paid the same whether they actually instruct students in the essence of the discipline they are supposed to be teaching during instructional time, or just hang out with kids during instructional time.

More liberty for individual teachers in how they attract students and how they negotiate for their own salary would benefit the better teachers. A teacher with a reputation for effective instruction would attract more students as both the students and their parents would know the reputation. Input from the "customers" (the students and parents) could offset administrative bias. Unions will not let that happen. There is great wisdom from George Bernard Shaw when he says: "Liberty means responsibility. That is why most men dread it".

If it were possible to assess knowledge per dollar, we could see how well teachers are teaching. Teachers are paid to be physically present in a school but what counts is how much knowledge the students are absorbing. In a sense, standardized testing measures knowledge per dollar. If the average student from Teacher A scores 85% correct in a standardized test, while students from Teacher B score 60%, it would be expected that Teacher A was more effective, provided the two groups of students has similar academic backgrounds and were from the same neighborhood, thus the same socioeconomic background.

If students could sign up for the teacher of their choice, better teachers would attract more students. When administrators assign teachers to the students, the students are getting whatever was given to them. Imagine if you went to the new car dealer and everyone paid the same price, but the dealer gave some customers a Mercedes, others a Chevy and others a 1974 Pinto with primer on the hood, sky blue paint on the quarter panels and a brown door taken from a scrap metal dealer.

Most teachers are not overpaid, but when employees are lumped with a group of people, there is a risk that they will be judged according to the perception of the laziest in the profession. To look at the laziest teacher in the profession, is to know they are grossly overpaid. Unions perhaps fear that the goal of management is a desire to force the most uncompensated work from a person as possible. Management may think the goal of unions is to take the most and give the least. In private industry, competition allows for some degree of normalization. A good product sells better than a bad product. In education, the tragedy is that students do not know if they are getting a good or bad education. Often teachers with low standards for themselves and their students are the most popular, as they represent a portion of the day which is wasted for the student: no learning, no homework, and no effort. The student thinks a free A is great until they get to college, and they cannot compete against other, better educated students. For that reason, if students were able to sign up for teachers of their choice, it would be important that some form of objective data indicating growth objectives of students was available.

Ultimately, the mark of a good teacher is a person who allows students to move forward and be competitive against future classmates when performance is more important, as it is during college.

Being again reminded of George Bernard Shaw when considering a teachers' union, he wrote: "The reasonable man adapts himself to the world; the unreasonable one persists in trying to adapt the world to himself. Therefore all progress depends on the unreasonable man." Taking on the establishment should be done when a person feels comfortable that their message is in the best interest of society as a whole. Still, in such cases, the fight against the establishment becomes tiresome, as not only does the status quo benefit the establishment members who have already benefitted from it, but the ambitious person sees their own wisdom in accepting rather than challenging the establishment, even if the establishment is wrong. The trials of the progressives, when compared to the comfort and ease of the acquiescent, become proof positive to the acquiescent of their own wisdom in ignoring the wrongs of a situation. Imagine a teacher making the remark: "This school will never tolerate more than mediocrity, so I never try". If that person sees another teacher giving their best effort only to be punished for it, they would not object, as their opinion was validated.

Something I know from boxing is that when you are close enough to your opponent to hit him, he is close enough to hit back. An individual teacher taking a shot at a union is like an ant taking a shot at Evander Holyfield. It is hard to change the system, but worth the effort to discuss areas where improvements can occur because the children are worth it.

My frustration with teachers who do not give their best effort to kids has been exaggerated by memories of often standing four to eight watches in the Coast Guard. To explain: When standing watches at sea, your watch times occur twice per day. If you are standing the 4-8 watch, it means you wake up at 3 am to be ready to share a joint patrol at 3:45. 4 am to 8 am is then your watch time. When your watch ends at 8am, the work day has begun, so you join in. When the work day ends, it is time to begin the 4-8 pm watch, after which you will hit the rack at 9 pm, anticipating that next 3 am wake up call.

Having such a background, it is difficult to enter a professional environment with twenty two year olds who are fresh out of college, and working for the first time in their lives. They are then instructed that to be accepted by the union, they must leave at 2:30, and they should know that their prep time is considered a break period. These ten month employees are making 40-50 thousand dollars per year, and they work in a country where the annual cost of remedial classes for college students is 7 billion dollars (Scott-Clayton, Judith & Crosta, Peter, & Belfield, Clive, 2012; Improving The Targeting Of Treatment: Evidence From College Remediation; National Bureau of Economic Research). If they absorb the work ethic thrust upon them, they will eventually reach a point where, after a long career, they are making $80,000 plus per year, having never worked hard. They will believe they deserve the income they receive, and may possibly never even concern themselves with such issues as there being up to 90% remediation rates in certain colleges (Barra, Kobus, 2012), or the fact that it is not uncommon for colleges to experience higher rates of loan defaults than graduations (Wang, Stephanie; 2013, Report: Loan default rates exceed graduation rates at Vincennes, Ivy Tech; IndyStar.com) Thankfully, many teachers do not follow that route, but any who do represent too many.

A good union is both an advocate for proper compensation for the employees and proper job performance from the employees. A good union wants a proper constitution in place which spreads leadership opportunities throughout the school and shows respect to all members. A dysfunctional union becomes a self serving machine to provide power to a few select members who form their own oligarchy. They retain their power by abusing the few who question their tactics, then benefit from the indifference of the many.

Are Americans more docile than they once were? The American Revolution began for, among other reasons, a tax of 3 pence per pound on tea. Union teachers pay (in my state) $1,100 dollars per year to the union. We do not complain. Perhaps we should not, if union support allows a public school teacher to earn over $1,000 more than a comparable private school teacher, the investment pays off for the individual. The issue then becomes a concern for how the union affects education as a whole. If there are 100 employees in a school, each paying full dues, then the school district is funneling $100,000 of tax money through the staff into the union. Does that expense truly benefit the students? If union behaviors are hurting the students in a school, someone needs to speak out, but the only ones who have the necessary view of what is going on are the union members. Conflict occurs in unions for many reasons, but due to the gang like mentality of some union leaders, there are no qualms with trying to destroy the career of a person who speaks out against the union.

To work in a field where everyone basically will be hired back year after year, may create an impression that there would be no internal squabbles, as people would be pleased with their good fortune. There are squabbles and much worse. Perhaps it is a result of being around young people too much and thinking that the behaviors they exhibit are normal for everyone, maybe it is just petty jealousies, truth be told, I do not know why some teachers behave the way they do. The best way to approach conflict is to face it head on, confront it and hope for resolution. At the very least it can be brought to the surface. There are teachers who could never last one shift in a minimum wage job who have spent decades in a school because they have tenure and perform at the most minimal level tolerable. A woman once made a disturbing comment in my presence: I've got a job for life as long as I don't have sex with a kid. I do not know that any child has ever learned an academic fact from the woman, but last I heard, she still has a job, so I guess she is holding down the fort on her one standard.

There are a great many excellent teachers who follow the rule: "Never go in the faculty room, only talk to other teachers when you have to, and stay in your classroom during breaks". Sounds odd, but this is true. They do not want to be a part of what goes on in the break room. Unfortunately, they are often some of the better people in the district. Their influence could provide a pleasant seasoning to the atmosphere in the school. Their absence from the field leaves people of lesser character with a greater degree of influence on the staff. I enjoy a summer position with some very dedicated teachers. When we are on break together, the art teachers discuss art, the English teachers discuss literature, and everyone has knowledge to share. I love spending lunch time with those people and only wish all school lunch rooms could function in the same way. There is a great deal to learn when educators share their expertise.

When the best and the brightest stay uninvolved, it allows less capable people to run the show. Their credo is "Play the game and cover your tracks". People who truly live that credo do not understand that there are times when a person with conviction refuses to "play the game" precisely because there is something of importance that needs to be faced. For the "Play the game" types, they hope to see the people who will confront problems fail. Failure of those who propose a paradigm shift when needed, reinforces a sense of wisdom in those who do not face problems. In education, the types of things that sometimes need to be faced head on include policies which are deleterious to the welfare of the children. Educators need to care more about the welfare of the students than they care about their own jobs. The policies that often need to be confronted do not need to be type written, published, dictates from the school. Often, they are the unwritten guidelines created by and maintained by staff members with pull in the district.

During a teachers first few years (prior to receiving tenure), their safest place is in the arms of the local union. Hopefully it is a healthy union, but it could be a dysfunctional union run by goons. By ingratiating themselves to such people, these non-tenured teachers will have support when they come up for tenure.

I have seen teachers who never have been, and never will become the teachers they might otherwise have become, simply because they accepted the embrace of a district's union. Now, I do not intend to characterize union teachers as goons with baseball bats, patrolling the docks or wharves of a port town like some kind of bad stereotype of a longshoreman's union. Their baseball bats are scurrilous gossip and the willingness to tell lies in packs.

Not playing the game means a teacher sometimes put his or her career in an uncomfortable place. "Do not play the game" is a hard thing to say, and a near impossible thing to convince others of, but if teachers think of it from a slightly different perspective, caring only about the welfare of the students provides them an explanation for their behavior should they ever be called to the carpet. Staying employable outside of education is another courage booster that most teachers could use.

With many pressures on teachers and many different views of what it takes to be a good teacher, it can be hard to accurately state what a good teacher is. Returning to H.L. Mencken: "A man who knows a subject so thoroughly, a man so soaked in it that he eats it, sleeps it and dreams it—this man can always teach it with success, no matter how little he knows of technical pedagogy". We need men and women like that in the classroom.

One burden we must overcome at this point in our history is our history to this point. If you consider our current populace, we grew up during an era when we were spending our parents' and grandparents wealth. We advanced into an age where we are spending our children's and grandchildren's future wealth through unchecked borrowing, thus people expect to receive more than they really earn. We have now burned through all the wealth accumulated during the post World War II generation, and have indebted our children's children to a tune of 17 trillion dollars. By desiring to earn every penny we receive, we can give to others our professional services, while receiving our salaries. Merely being physically present on the job site is not productivity. When I talk to friends in industry who complain about a new employee who exerts a minimum of effort and feels comfortable with that, I can imagine the types of teachers who educated that young person. An expectation of reward without exerting effort can be the result of spending days on end with a teacher who gives free periods and study hall days as a reward for not misbehaving during previous free periods.

My first experience with union work was in college, loading trucks on the midnight shift (12 am-9am). After several years of having to drop out periodically, while working for 3 dollars and change per hour, it was a joy to work in a venue with support for the workers. A good friend of mine named Kenny introduced me to his boss and put me in a position to finally continue straight through school with no more withdrawals. I am grateful for that to this day. The salary for loading trucks was $13/hour. To a broke college kid, it was a fortune. I would exert myself to my best abilities, unloading 4 trucks per night and not thinking anything about it, good or bad.

After a while, the older, established teamsters would not help me when there was a heavy pallet to move. We, part-time workers used the pallet jacks, the full-timers used the forklifts. Some pallets were over a thousand pounds, too heavy for a pallet jack or Johnson bar. I would walk over and ask for help. They were always very nice to me. "Sure thing Danny, I'll be right there". After 20 or 30 minutes, they would show up, other times, not until after break. Still, they were never mean. They were just slow enough in helping me to adjust my pace. Finally, Kenny pulled me aside and explained that the proper pace (according to the union) was to unload two trucks per night. It was interesting to me how they had chosen to pace me. The funny thing is, that there was never a time when anyone was being mean to me. The "leaders" in a teachers' union can be vicious. When they attack, it is not about slowing down someone's pace at work. They seek to destroy careers. On the loading dock, I used to always wear old high top canvas Chuck Taylor's. They had holes through the canvass on the sides, and holes through the rubber on the bottom. The one forklift operator, Frank, would almost never help me move a pallet, but he would ask me every night for my shoe size, so he could get me boots. I always declined, but found the dichotomy of his actions endearing. On one hand, he was not going to allow me to work rapidly, but on the other hand, he had a genuine concern for my welfare.

On a loading dock, there is a form of logic in the union mentality behind setting a pace, leading to a set price for each unloaded truck. Despite not being fully in agreement with it, there is a logic behind it. Having read "The Jungle" by Upton Sinclair, a person develops concern with the management mindset of taking the best a worker has to offer, then discarding that worker. If you have never read "The Jungle", there is a character named Jurgis Rudkus. He is youthful, powerfully built, and able to out work any other laborer. When a shift of workers was selected, he would always be the first chosen. Over time, the expenditure of his strength in harsh conditions wore him down. He eventually became less desirable. He was no longer the strongest, he became disposable. In a perfect world, people would give their very best at every point in their career and when they could no longer keep the pace they had offered to their employers in their youth, the employer would honor the years of service from that employee by finding a less stressful function for them in the company. Administrators need to be the balance between the games unions can play and the reality that workers need spokespersons.

It would be ideal if people always gave their best effort, and we lived in a world where after decades of loyal service to a company, there were allowances made for those who could no longer give the effort they once did.

Since local union leadership positions are time intensive, there is a danger that they will be taken and held by the lower quality professionals who are not spending much time educating students in the first place. Good unions should generate leadership opportunities for all members, and cycle through various people in leadership roles as a way of involving the multiple mindsets that make up a staff.

In the autobiography of Frederick Douglass, he mentions how a few motivated workers in the north could complete the work of many abused slaves in the south. Frederick was one of those motivated workers. He thrived and prospered in his new environment. Among the famous abolitionists of his day, none is more inspiring than Frederick Douglass. He escaped slavery in 1838, rose to become an editor and orator. He was a welcome guest in Lincoln's White House and a world renowned champion for liberation. His story is one of great achievement in the face of adversity. None of us can imagine today what his life must have been like. Why would anyone expect a slave to do more than go through the motions of their day to day duties? With educators, who are guaranteed employment year after year, just going through the motions is inexcusable. You may think a person would feel gratitude for such security and work hard. Some do, some others instead develop a sense of entitlement.

It would be very difficult to implement a rewards based salary structure in education. We could pay teachers based on number of students who enrolled in their classes. Taking 6 classes per day as an example and $12,000 per year as the average tuition rate in a public school, we could divide it up as $2,000 per year per class. Students would always need math, science, English, and history. They would then have various electives they could take each year: computers, cooking, wood shop, etc. Of the $2,000 per year, per class, $500 could be shaved off of the top for materials, infrastructure, heating oil, administration, etc.

That would leave $1,500 per student per teacher. A teacher with 100 students per year would then be earning $150,000 per year, with $50,000 available for supporting infrastructure. The more students interested in taking that teacher's class, the more that teacher would earn. A teacher with 110 students interested in taking their class in a given year would work a longer day, but would earn $165,000 for that year. In other words, if benefits were assigned to any teacher who has four sections of students, as being a full time teacher, but based on enrollment a teacher could work up to seven or eight periods per day, the extra work would benefit the teacher financially, and benefit students who could have access to better quality teachers. A danger is that if students had their own choice of classes to take, they would be tempted to take classes with lower quality teachers who offered higher grades for less work. This mindset sometimes appears in colleges where students will rate different professors based on ease of the course. That scenario represents a concern which would need to be addressed.

In major league baseball, a .250 hitter is valued less than a .300 hitter. In this sense, standardized tests would tilt the scales in favor of the more competent teachers. If a student needs a certain score on their end of course competency test, he or she will be more inclined to take the teacher with the higher level of success. What about the inherent abilities of students in different districts? Teachers can shine in any environment, not by being compared with a national average, but by being compared with the averages within their district. New York City rates teachers based on how their group of students performed on standardized tests when compared to the year before. In other words, if your group of students had a collective score of 212 on the previous year's science assessment, and this year, they have an average score collectively of 215, that teacher positively impacted the students' learning. A teacher with students who, the year before scored 245, but then scored 237, saw an achievement loss despite the fact that the 237 earned by the second group is a higher score than the 215 earned by the first group.

There are always going to be teachers who would rather focus on the most gifted students, as those students require the least effort, and achieve at a rate which reflects well on whomever their teacher is. Therefore, rather than have higher quality teachers avoid students who are less gifted in a particular area just so they can maintain a higher "batting average", students could have access to teachers of various skill levels by having teachers teach some high level classes and some low level classes.

"Teacher choice" is a much more feasible reality than school choice. Over time, as evidence mounted regarding which teachers were capable, and which were not, the least capable teachers would be phased out of districts. There are a great many ways we could tinker with education to improve the quality of it. It can be an onerous task as Michelle Rhee knows.

The Bee Eater

Michelle Rhee began her teaching career in the Harlem Park section of Baltimore and encountered the specter of failure for the first time in her life. She was a Harvard graduate struggling to make 8 year olds listen to her as her class tumbled out of control. An 8 year old does not think; Wow, I am learning from a person with an Ivy League degree! They cannot appreciate what they have in front of them. Unfortunately, too few adults have the ability to realize what is of value in a classroom as well. When Michelle was ready to pack it in, her father told her to get back in the classroom "You've never failed at anything. You're not a quitter". (The Bee Eater, Richard Whitmire, page 32). That story reminds me of an encounter Mickey Mantle had with his father when Mickey was ready to quit baseball after a demotion to the minors as a rookie.

There are times when someone has given it all they have and are ready to throw in the towel. As a teacher, it is important to notice those times and give a little push and a pat on the shoulder.

Michelle Rhee's almost giving up as a teacher is logical, a person who knows how to generate success can become very frustrated by the machinations in school systems which make it difficult for top quality employees to achieve at a level commensurate with their own efforts. Her approach to leadership while School's Chancellor in Washington D.C. is also logical. Unfortunately, the classroom is not always a place people go to when they are motivated to achieve excellence in their chosen profession. It is a profession which, when done right, can require 10 and 12 hour days. When done wrong, requires 6 hours of little or no effort. The question is how to keep salaries at an appropriate level while still giving the kids the most they can get for the price. Consider nutrition: If you want a full belly, you can buy junk food for $1 per item. If you want health food, the price will be much more expensive. If you look at nutrient per dollar, the health food is the better bargain. If you look at quantity, the junk food is the better value. The key is to discern which teachers are providing their students with mental nutrition, and which teachers are merely filling a desk. When we discuss teacher salaries, we should think in terms of "knowledge per dollar" provided to each student.

Think in terms of dollars per day per child. A low quality teacher making $50,000/year can be compared to a better quality teacher making $60,000/year. Suppose it is an elementary school, and they work with the same group of kids all day. They teach 24 students per classroom for 180 days. 24 students x 180 days= 4,320 instructional days per year to the students. The cost of a low quality teacher is $50,000/4,320 = $11.57 per day per child for instruction. A higher quality teacher making $60,000/4,320 = $13.89 per day. In order to save two dollars per day, there are administrators who are happier with 180 days of study halls and wasted time, than 180 days of mind enriching education. By the way, as a rebuke to those who call teachers babysitters, good luck finding a babysitter for $13.89/day.

When friends in industry complain about their difficulties finding young people willing to work hard at a first job (even one that pays well), it is hard not to consider how, for so many years, some young people are taught to feel comfortable doing nothing except showing up for school every day without really trying to achieve at a high level. We see the importance of quality educators discussed in Michelle Rhee's accomplishments. She took a group of students who were scoring in the 13th percentile on standardized tests, and within two years, they were scoring in the 90th percentile. Teachers can be petty, and I am sure she was not universally applauded by her fellow professionals. So what? If Jim Thome hits 50 homeruns in a season, is he supposed to feel bad for the guy who hit 1 homerun and is batting .210? No he is not. More importantly, the guy hitting 1 homerun with a .210 batting average would not be able to gather up the other .200 hitters and form a union where no one was supposed to hit 50 homeruns. If those players did not want to look bad, they would have to perform better. If they could not perform better, it certainly would be no knock on their humanity, just an indication to step aside, let someone else have their turn, and the .200 hitter could find a profession where they would be more successful.

My mixed feelings on unions bears explaining. There was a reasonable logic behind why those teamsters did not want me unloading 4 trucks per night way back when I was in college. They wanted a set pace, and a set price per truck. In a school system, the union leaders who demand that all teachers do the minimum work for the most pay bring disgrace to the profession. Teachers only have one chance to help kids. The amount of help provided to children should not be leveled off at some low quality teacher's arbitrary opinion of "enough". There are teachers who are verbally abused for offering to stay late and help kids. This makes no sense. Staying late to help kids on a regular basis is very little to ask from adults who have off from work for one week at Christmas, one week at Easter and who have two months off for summer vacation.

Hard core union leaders perceive that a hard working teacher puts pressure on other teachers to work hard. In such a situation, the union should simply applaud the hard working teacher, but stick to their guns when it comes time to renegotiate a contract. They can accept that teacher X offers a great deal to kids, but it will not be made mandatory in the contract.

Working hard for kids when it is not mandated, is the only way to truly let the children know that they are worth the teacher's effort. Then the child knows that they are cared about. A child who has been cared for is more likely to grow into an adult who cares for others.

Dorothy Law Nolte wrote a poem "Children Learn What They Live". She correlates good input with good output, bad input with bad output. By the numbers, it certainly seems that way when the law of averages is applied. What may surprise you is the resilience of kids. Many kids who receive bad input actually turn around and bless the world with good output. This is not permission for adults to input anything bad into a child's psyche, it is just an acknowledgement of the ability children have to overcome bad influences. An astute teacher can identify children who receive bad input. Those children need good advice, a caring environment and positive role models.

Each teacher does have something good to provide to their students, and there should be no demands made which turn teachers into uniform, interchangeable parts. Rather than seek uniformity, teachers should be like a field of wildflowers, each distinct, each offering something unique to the school environment. Teachers should not have the uniformity of a neatly groomed lawn, where everyone has been mowed down to an indistinct structure. Neither administrators, nor union leaders should do the mowing. It is hard to find an answer to the question of how to get the best education for the least money. Clearly, the money is there, it just needs to be distributed properly. The goal should be to get the best education possible at the proper price. When private schools that are sending kids to Ivy League institutions are paying teachers in the mid 40's, and public schools with 50% literacy rates are paying teachers 90K, it is difficult to encourage the 90K union teacher to trust the caprices of the free market.

Regardless of feelings on teacher salaries, unless the economy itself heals, there will be less and less money available to support education. Our current rate of unemployment is something we all should have seen coming for twenty years. Initially, we (in our arrogance) felt we could ship overseas, the jobs we were "too important" to do ourselves, factory labor, etc. Well, once the production facilities were all overseas, it was only time until the higher level positions followed. Are we better off taking advantage of labor from countries where workers are exploited? Personally, I am fond of having unskilled labor jobs available in an economy. Such jobs allowed me to pay for my college. People will not want to work their entire lives in such a position, but it is better to work while building skills for a career than to borrow tuition money hoping the education for which a person becomes indebted will later bear fruit.

In the article: *Report: Loan default rates exceed graduation rates at Vincennes, Ivy Tech*: "Ivy Tech's graduation rate at 5 percent in 2009 and 4 percent in 2010, against 20.2 percent of students who entered loan repayment in 2009 and defaulted within three years (Wang, 2013) illustrates a few problems. High schools are not preparing students to be successful at the college level, and with fewer jobs available, funding is not being earned, but rather borrowed. If those loans do not bear fruit later by providing the debtor with the skills necessary to earn the money to repay such loans, default is the likely option. As a nation, our current debt exceeds 100% of our GDP. We do not need more debt being accrued which does not turn around later and create sufficient wealth to offset the debt incurred. Our debt is not a comfortable debt. Japan as a nation has more debt than we do, but their debt is mostly internal, comprised of bonds sold to citizens. We have a great deal of foreign debt.

Shifting production jobs overseas carries with it another moral dilemma. If we feel our workers deserve a standard of living that provides some minimal level of comfort, how can we feel comfortable taking advantage of people without that option? Hard work deserves rewards. Any teacher can see that some students struggle academically, but often those students are the most willing to work hard. There are also students who struggle academically because they refuse to work hard. Those students who are willing to work hard should have jobs available to them when they graduate from high school. It does not matter whether or not those are the most glamorous positions. To a working man, it is the carrying of this own weight which is the minimum he will accept from himself. Regarding the people who struggle because they refuse to work hard, leading a horse to water is enough.

Since leading a horse to water is really, in this case, about leading a person to a job opportunity, it becomes important that jobs remain available. The greater picture of job opportunities across the nation goes beyond the scope of a book about education. Public schools are run based on availability of tax revenue, therefore, the existence of that revenue requires that people in town have employment. In that natural resources are the raw materials upon which industry can run, we must as a nation protect those resources.

Things are more complicated than they were when Native Americans ruled this continent. The words of the Shawnee warrior Tecumseh encompass an ideal vision of how people might cohabitate this planet.

"Sell a country! Why not sell the air, as well as the earth? Did not the Great Spirit make them all for the use of his children?"

Living now in a world of private ownership, there is increased need to understand a responsibility to all of mankind when natural resources are utilized. Small organic farms and responsible aquaculture are two ways to preserve our natural resources. However, once schools enter the picture, the production side of the economy has already made its contribution. That production is a concern in light of the rapid increase in national debt. It is one thing for school revenue to be tied to taxes collected from effective production processes, quite another for it to be based on taking a share of borrowed money.

In schools, the tax money is entrusted to the staff in that building, and distributed according to the priorities of the administrators and unions. Those priorities should be based on what is best for children. When a school has an opening for a position, the choice may come down to: a personal friend of the administrator doing the hiring or a very well qualified candidate. The best candidate should get the job, however, there are times when the friend will be given the job, and a town's tax money will be spent not to best provide for the needs of children, but to place a supporter of the administrator into the mix, chalking up a personal debt to an individual when that individual gave nothing of their own personal wealth to the recipient; they merely allocated tax money to a friend. Likewise, unions will often renegotiate contracts in a way that throws a great deal of money at the step of a long time union player who is soon to retire, and therefore wants their pension based on the largest salary possible. Unions may also choose to minimize the salary on the step of a person who is not part of their clique. Punishing people financially is a typical way adults in unions bully staff members.

Unions are Bad, Unions are Good

The value of unions lies in the realm of unions being organizations which encourage teachers to support each other in our field. Working through contract renegotiations, and being organized to perform volunteer work to help students are two areas where unions have value.

If you do not think that a union clique can influence the whole atmosphere of a school, you are wrong. When unions encourage excellence, administrators can do so comfortably. The great disconnect lies in the fact that people who expect excellence of themselves are less likely to melt into packs. People who are drawn to packs are most likely the lower quality individuals in the first place. Therefore, if teachers' unions are to properly represent the best of this professions, the higher quality individuals must be willing to participate in them. As Plato said: "A person who refuses to participate in politics chooses to be governed by his inferiors". The danger lies in what a dysfunctional union may do to a person who tries to influence a union in the right direction.

All people are equal in terms of their humanity, and should be treated as such at all times. That does not mean that people have equal authority and responsibility in the work place. There are people who are in a position where respect should be given and deserved. When people lose sight of the equality of all people, decisions can be made which are of value to none.

Unions can be places where the worst character traits in humans are made manifest; but they can, when properly led, shine like a light well beyond their requirement to advocate for teachers.

A union can be a conduit through which fundraiser activities for scholarships can be organized. It can be a source of collegiality between staff members, it can celebrate teacher accomplishments, and much more. A healthy level of involvement by all members based first and foremost on a commitment to the best interests of students, with the emphasis being placed on ensuring fairness in the way teachers are treated is the recipe for a union with an appropriate raison d'etre.

CHAPTER FOURTEEN

Reasons for Optimism

"Do not let yourself be tainted with a barren skepticism."

~ Louis Pasteur

After wading through the stories the media feeds us every day, we need to redirect our focus. Looking into the lives of people who do what is right when they are motivated only by their own conscience, you will see that there is room for optimism. It is best seen from close up, and best seen in the lives of individuals you know personally.

Watching kids joyfully playing and seeing adults cordially interacting, makes for a boring news story, which is why 99.99% of what goes on in life does not end up on the news. A couple at an Al Fresco bistro, parents walking a stroller, a group of teenage boys playing sports, are as much a part of the American fabric today as they were when Norman Rockwell was capturing similar moments on canvas.

Educators get to do more than witness society, they get to influence it. It is a great trust, and a trust to be handled with care. All of society benefits when children are nurtured to be intelligent and caring.

Intelligent people of character are less inclined to countenance wrong indifferently. Consider the TSA. To see a 90 year old woman forced to remove her Depends undergarments before being permitted to board an airplane should be enough to sound an alarm. Our ability to vote is the key to our having a say in this country. Increasingly, it seems we are always left with a choice between candidates who are bad or worse and we lack the knowledge to discern which candidate will do the least damage to our country.

The new direction must come from the youth. We need to let excellence flourish and help it grow. We need to reinforce young people when they do what is good, noble and honorable. Sometimes a pat on the back is the best thing we can give a kid. Schools do not even want an adult to touch a child in the slightest way. A young boy from the autistic program in my school delivers the papers everyday. Getting a hug from him makes MY day.

Adults need to be very careful in how they show affection to students, but it is good to let kids know they are cared for. It is also important to share success stories featuring people who have overcome hardships.

To better encourage students to seek excellence in themselves, we need role models who embody what it takes to succeed in life and overcome adversity.

Gac

With that thought in mind, consider a small portion of an article published by the associated press on May 13th, 2012. It embodies the day to day character which defines an ordinary type of heroism. Heroism need not be battlefield bravery. It can be day to day commitment to improvement in oneself and in one's society.

NEW YORK—For years, Gac Filipaj mopped floors, cleaned toilets and took out trash at Columbia University.

A refugee from war-torn Yugoslavia, he eked out a living working for the Ivy League school. But today was payback time: The 52-year-old janitor donned a cap and gown to graduate with a bachelor's degree in classics.

For Filipaj, the degree comes after years of studying late into the night in his Bronx apartment, where he'd open his books after a 2:30-11 p.m. shift as a "heavy cleaner"—his job title. Before exam time or to finish a paper, he'd pull all-nighters, then go to class in the morning and then to work.

A college education is the ticket to leadership roles in society; it is a way to advance into management positions. Wouldn't it be great if we could all have bosses like Gac Filipaj?

He is a man who believes knowledge is wealth. We need to reassess what wealth is. Is it the stockpile of merchandise we store in our closets? No. Knowledge is a form of wealth, but the greatest currency we spend is time, the minutes and hours of our lives. The time spent with our children, friends and families. Money is needed in a much smaller quantity when we are satiated by a walk in the park, time spent with books in a library, and time spent playing hide and go seek with the children in our lives. Gac mentioned his love of reading the classics in the article. Classic literature often focuses on heroic figures of fact or fiction. My heroes have always been men and women who work hard and take care of their families. Gac does not live a life of fame and fortune; his is a life that any of us can live, provided we have the right attitude.

Still Waters

During the summer of 2012, I was greatly blessed to be able to travel with a group of young people to visit the Navajo Nation in New Mexico and Arizona. It was the most emotionally refreshing journey of my lifetime. The young people were unpaid and needed to raise the money for the trip on their own. Once those young people arrived at the school on the reservation, their commitment to the children was remarkable. There was no bickering for seniority, no desideration for more free time, or less responsibility. These students filled every need the young campers had. They served as coaches during sports camp, teachers during VBS, assistants during arts and crafts time, cooks at lunch time, nurses when a child got hurt and laborers during our time working on service projects. They were loved and hugged by the campers. After 20 years as a teacher, I was never more uniformly surrounded by educators. "Educator" is a term I use with respect. There are times when a teacher is not an educator, they are merely a school district employee. These young people were educators. There was a feeling of overwhelming pride being associated with them.

It is because of young people like those I worked with that I can feel optimistic about our country. They were joyful in repose and hardworking at all other times. There was more in them than just a desire to enjoy the here and now. They earned their keep, helped others, and treated each other with kindness and respect.

While visiting the reservation, we had the opportunity to see what wealth of spirit looks like in the midst of material poverty. Many of the locals were in possession of a type of good cheer which was contagious. Yet there are still land and water rights issues to be contended with for Native Americans, issues of poverty far more severe than anything most Americans can understand. We do have issues to resolve within our own communities, but it is imperative that we also find ways to repair the damage we have inflicted on native cultures.

The type of hardship being endured should be defined. Financial hardship does not always mean emotional hardship. The Navajo I met were kind and loving, with tight knit families and ready smiles. They live in a region where every evening brings a beautiful sunset, and every night provides a celestial show of supreme beauty. A comment that brought home my feelings about that trip was made by an "Anglo" who had the best of intentions. Navajos refer to Americans of European decent as "Anglos". The gentleman met our group at Window Rock, and complimented us for the work we were doing. He had stayed in the house where we were being accommodated. After mentioning how much the children appreciated our time with them, he applauded our willingness to stay in a house with few amenities, and various drawbacks such as mice and spiders in the walls, etc. etc. His feelings about our house were the same as my own upon seeing it for the first time. Walls were broken, eaves were hanging from rotten beams, and the desperate need for paint was apparent on every inch inside and outside. Yet, by the end of the first day, I believed that house to be one of the finest places I had ever stayed.

Our hosts were a couple named Jeff and DeAnne of Three Springs Ministries. Every day, Jeff would perform repair duties for the facility, while DeAnne prepared delicious meals for 22 people and scores of children. At night, a couple of young ladies (Amy and Bethany) would play music. Our boys and girls would be on the basketball court every night playing with many of the local children who would come by the school, and everyone was courteous to each other. The happiness a person can enjoy in the absence of material wealth when everyone is courteous to each other is ineffable.

On one night, an unexpected comedy occurred. A few counselors were having a conference on the front porch, and the boys in my group wanted to go out for a walk, but did not want to disrupt the conversation. By the time I noticed what they were doing to egress, they were already on the roof of the building. They were trying to get down from the second floor, and considering how best to jump. I poked my head out of the window, and to the one boy who was getting ready to jump, I gave the instructions: "first land on your feet, then your hands, then roll. Feet, hands, roll, feet hands roll". To another young man, who was still looking for a more normal descent, I advised him to reach out for a branch and shimmy down the tree. As they reached the ground, Jeff (our leader) arrived, and spent some time talking with them. Being a leader myself, I was a bit chagrined to be seen by Jeff, as I was not dissuading their actions but giving them the instructions: "feet, hands, roll".

Straddling Two Worlds

I am very encouraged by such young people, and could not be happier than I am when around such people. They make me hope that I will be a member of two straddle generations. If you are are in your 40's, like me, you are part of a straddle generation. We are part of a straddle generation, in that we were born during the dying days of one era in our country, and currently live in a different era.

Television does too much in defining America. Since it does, it helps define the notion of a "straddle generation". For children of the 1970s, *The Waltons* and *Little House on the Prairie* were full of wholesome values. We old folks in our forties have one foot in that generation. Today, the list of entertainers and programs which endorse all forms of vulgarity is too long to provide. We have one foot in this generation. Hence, we straddle a generation where values were encouraged if not universally accepted, and a generation where acceptance of vulgarity is common.

If I could see this next generation take on the values of those teens I spent my summer with, I would have the greatest hope for the future of this country. There could be nothing better than to see us step away from what we have become and return to the values we once held.

Personally knowing literally thousands of young people with great character is my reason for optimism, seeing how even good kids can be twisted by casuistic adults with insidious intentions is my reason for concern. Optimism must bear fruit, which means planting, tending and caring for the source of that fruit.

CHAPTER FIFTEEN

Wish List

"How wonderful it is that nobody need wait a single moment before starting to improve the world."

~ Anne Frank

Having shared so many concerns, and perhaps not enough solutions, leaves a need to discuss how education might improve.

1.) Once teachers enter the profession, they should take at least one class per year specifically in their subject towards an advanced degree. Too often, teacher training is about sharing a continental breakfast before spending a day complaining about conditions in schools. Learning is a life-long process. Students are best served by teachers who are experts in an academic discipline rather than pedagogy.

2.) Limit the salary for administrators by considering not only their desire to move up the pay scale, but also in accordance with the amount of time they have spent in the profession. An administrator with a minimal time in the classroom will have little to offer an experienced teacher. A person in their sixth year in the profession deserves more money as an administrator than a person in their sixth year teaching; however, if the salary differential allows for a doubling in pay by making that jump, people will enter administration for the money rather than because they have anything to offer other teachers.

3.) Create a tiered system of compensation. If one teacher is in a discipline which requires no grading of homework and another teacher needs to work an extra 4 hours per day doing paper work, that adds up to an additional 720 hours of work (a full 18 weeks of work during the school year). That additional 18 weeks of work is an unfair burden, and moreover, it often keeps the hardest working teachers from pursuing advancement into administration due to time constraints which prevent them from taking administration courses. This leaves too many leadership positions available for people who have never really struggled to transmit academic excellence to students. Often the way teachers balance this amongst themselves is by academic teachers choosing to not assign homework. In that way, the teacher of an academic subject can also leave at dismissal with the kids; however, the children never learn the study skills they will need in order to succeed in college. If teachers are to focus time on paper work, the grading of students' homework in an effective manner is more important than writing amazing lesson plans. That time commitment needs to somehow be acknowledged.

4.) Dismantle the current union system. It is top heavy, expensive and broken. Union affiliations should always be welcome; however, due again to unfair work schedules in schools, often it is the teachers who exert the most minimal effort for students who end up running local unions decade after decade. If term limits are needed in Congress, they are also needed in school unions. Unions need to choose which sword they want to wield. Either they want teachers to be well paid and well respected professionals, or they want teachers to have short work days during short work years. The tragedy is that those teachers who understand the importance of the profession are already working very hard while being stereotyped with the low effort teachers. As previously mentioned, it is very easy for one teacher to literally put in 18 extra work weeks per year when compared to another teacher.

5.) Expel students who refuse to learn and who refuse to let other students learn. There are many arguments for keeping disruptive kids in school, and these arguments win the day if it were to happen that once the students were kept in school, they turned over a new leaf. An argument made is that if kids are kicked out of schools, they will then become problems on the streets. Well, what happens in areas where there are 50% drop out rates and a 10% expulsion rate would create a safer environment for the students who in turn would not drop out due to school violence? There would be fewer kids on the streets. Schools no longer deal with gum chewing as a major discipline issue. The violence in schools must end. In terms of education as a private industry, some teachers may choose to offer G.E.D. sessions at local libraries to students who were expelled, providing second chances for those kids and a heightened sense of the value of education. Teachers should work as hard as possible to help a student redirect his or her life, but once problems are too big for teachers to handle, the administrators need to make the tough decisions.

6.) Create term limits on school boards of education. Boards of education also become power bases for people who wish to feel important and who wish to hold the careers of others in their hands. The notion that any eighteen year old who lives in a particular town meets the requirements of being a board member is antiquated and needs to go. Also, all teachers in the school should, on a revolving basis, take turns being liaisons to the board of education. If there are 7 board members, that number can be supplemented by adding two teachers who serve a one year term as liaisons. If teachers do not have direct access to the board of education, all of the information board members receive will come from the administrators who have six figure jobs to protect. Board members should have some professional background to offer a school district. That background may be construction, education, law of other field, but schools need board members with something to offer. There are a great many good people in any town who want to serve. They should not have their opportunity denied them just because another member is going onto a tenth year in that seat.

7.) Teach kids and their parents that a C is not a horrible grade. Grade inflation is creating overconfidence and high remediation rates in colleges for students who were supposedly already prepared to enter college.

8.) Allow students and parents access to teacher evaluations. Whether it is the old system of one observation per year for tenured teachers, or newer systems requiring three to five observations per year, there is much more information to be gleaned by asking students and parents what they thought about teachers in addition to what the administrators think. Moreover, by opening up this type of system, schools get feedback from all parents, not just those who are the most vocal. Some people always need to be heard, and they are typically the outliers. Open up the ability to provide input to all students and their parents. I found a comment on a website very helpful, in that it opened my eyes to a perception of myself I had not considered. The student said: "Mr. Helm is a very nice guy… he genuinely cares about his students. His lessons are pretty difficult, as he expects that students know more about the topic than they do. Make sure you make appointments to see him outside of class… he is much better one and one or in a small group. Overall his lab is tough and he doesn't curve his exam grades." I had not thought I was going too fast in that course and I did not realize students knew less than I expected. That one comment helped me grow. It would be preferable to not get comments from a website, but rather just on a piece of paper, either way, the students I teach for 180 days have opinions which are more valuable than the opinion of the administrator who observed me a time or two, and is not trying to learn the subject from me. The student's opinion helped me grow as a teacher. The administrator's opinion impacts my job. Even the worst teacher can present a good lesson twice a year during their observations.

9.) Finally, and this is something for which others will need to take charge, our culture needs to heal, and we need to embrace things that are good and wholesome. Unfortunately, I do not know how to cause that change, I just know it needs to happen.

Woodrow Wilson was criticized for going beyond 10 suggestions for insuring world peace when World War I ended, so I will stay below ten suggestions for improving education.

CHAPTER SIXTEEN

Final Thoughts

"I am impelled, not to squeak like a grateful and apologetic mouse, but to roar like a lion out of pride in my profession."

~ John Steinbeck

Daniel Helm

"A great civilization is not conquered from without until it has destroyed itself from within." Will Durant studied civilizations across the scope of history and made this conclusion. We are currently a civilization which may destroy itself from within. The stand we must now make is a refusal to let ourselves be conquered from without while we concomitantly repair ourselves from within. For decades now, we have been influenced by those who espouse an absence of personal responsibility. It has been possible to absorb the consequences of these ideologies while we were in the process of squandering away the entirety of the wealth the nation had collected following our success in World War Two. Since that wealth has been lost, we have been able to maintain the same lifestyle by indebting our children, and then our grandchildren. We must now earn our keep, and we must be permitted to earn our keep by a government willing to provide to us the opportunities to realize our goals. That government must stop wasting the money we earn by being held accountable by a well informed populace.

Improving America requires providing Americans with opportunities to work hard at quality endeavors.

Gambling was recently introduced into my home area as a way to stimulate the economy. It was accepted as a good idea by many. However, gambling fits into the economic realm of being an enterprise which causes money to change hands, while offering no product at the end of a day's labor. Again, if a carpenter builds a house, at the end of the day, a family has shelter and the carpenter has a paycheck. At the end of a day, a farmer has fed his neighbors, and he has a paycheck. At the end of a day, a gambler has fleeced the unwitting, sending them back to their families with nothing, and the gambler has an incredibly fat paycheck in exchange for the emptiness he has dished out.

This news of gambling is notable in that it was heralded as good news. It is not good news. A former student of mine, who is a cancer survivor, spent her youth organizing fundraisers for other kids with cancer. She is a great kid and a brilliant student. After beating her own cancer, she was accepted into a college nursing program. She was then awarded a full college scholarship by the Philadelphia Eagles. That is good news! Good news is out there, and it needs to be celebrated. (Praising my former student is easy. Praising the Philadelphia Eagles is tough for a Giants fan, but they deserve it.)

There are so many issues on the table at this point in America's history, but we have always had crises to handle. Crises are overcome when people are willing to do the right thing. Sometimes we act as if merely doing the right thing is difficult. In 1945, as World War II came to an end, in a private poll 15 of 16 baseball owners opposed integration of the game (Ken Burns Baseball 6th inning). There was a voice of opposition to the practice of segregation. It was Branch Rickey, general manager of the Dodgers. Branch Rickey was willing to stand alone and integrate the game of baseball. I recommend you not be afraid of being alone. Be afraid of doing what is wrong. Every person in America has benefitted from the example of Jackie Robinson, not as an athlete, but as a man.

Character is never out of style. When Bill Bratton became the New York City police chief, he emphasized the broken window policy: A broken window in a building leads to more and more broken windows, leading to an undermining of the atmosphere in the neighborhood, leading to more severe societal issues as the neighborhood goes down hill. Therefore, when a window breaks, fix it. America is fixable, and the small things are important. Fixing the small things will eradicate or at least diminish the number of big things that need to be fixed.

When working to improve our country, let us remember the words of Jesse Jackson as he eulogized Jackie Robinson: "Jackie Robinson was immunized by God from catching the diseases he fought". We have so many great men and women in this country to honor and remember. We need only to do so more often. We need to fight the diseases of this country while not catching those diseases.

How can we avoid the diseases we fail to acknowledge as diseases? Often Americans are told not to judge. In a recent news story, a politician who likes to take inappropriate photographs of himself and e-mail them to young women was confronted by a voter. The politician belligerently demanded that the voter not judge him. This made me think: as a politician, isn't he asking people to judge him and judge his fitness to serve? I researched the Greek words for judge, and found variations of the original word. Katakrino was defined as judging by damning, while anakrino was defined as judging by properly scrutinizing. Americans must stop questioning their right to scrutinize changes in our culture. We are not always going to be the ones to condemn, but we must scrutinize what is going on in America and be courageous in voicing our opinions. Only by scrutinizing right and wrong can we do what is right.

Doing what is right often has little or no motivation beyond the altruistic nature of doing what is right, and the things we can do often seem too small.

Mother Teresa was a woman who knew the cost of doing what is right in a world where people often do what is wrong. There was a woman in my neighborhood who I greatly respected when I was growing up. That woman, who was a widow, not only raised her own children to be model citizens, but helped anyone else who was in need. In that she was a fan of Mother Teresa, I've always enjoyed reading about Mother Teresa. Closing this book with a quote from that wonderful woman serves as a reminder of what it is to be a teacher: "We can do no great things; only small things with great love".

Index

A

Adams, John 83
Abu Ghraib 108
Accused, The 129
ADHD 54
Aesop 55
AIDS 126
Alzheimer's 40
Al Qaeda 73
AP Classes 145
Arnold, Benedict 58
Arctic (Ocean) 55
Axon Terminal End Bulbs 24

B

Balls 10
Banks, Ernie 139
Banksy 67
Bergenfield School District 173
Biologist's Saint Patty's Day Song 125
Bloom's Taxonomy 60,61
Boards of Education 206
Boatswain Mate 56
Bobbitt, Lorena 31
Boys 30,32, 147
Brahe, Tycho 71
Bratton, Bill 211
Brimelow, Peter 175
Brokaw, Tom 137
Bullying 33,34,35
Bureau of Labor Statistics 32
Bush, George W 73

C

California 39
Canter, Lee 61
Carpenters 22,23, 64
Carpenter, Karen 118

Carter, Jimmy 11
Carver, George Washington 71
Cassata, Donna 90
Catholic Schools 18
CDC 126
Centers for Disease Control 40
Chamberlain, Joshua 18
Cheerleading 136
China 70, 80
Civil War 18, 85, 88, 137
Clayton, Judith Scott 59
CNN 35
Coast Guard (USCG) 55, 131, 178
Congress, 109th 27
Constitution 39, 83, 153
Continental Congress 85
Core Content Standards 25
Cosby Show 111
Costa Rica 98
Croce, Jim 123, 124
Custer, George 156

D

Daily News 37
Declaration of Independence 85
Deer Park 20
DeLaSalle car 79
Dempsey, Jack 130
Department of Education 11, 105
Detroit 79
Dideoxynucleic acids 62
DiMaggio, Joe 137

DNA 60, 70
Dodgers 211
Donald, David 89
Douglass, Frederick 185
Durant, Will 210
Drew, Charles Richard 72
Drop Out Rates 30

E

East Side High School 174
Eckert, Allan 89
Edelman, Marian 157
Einstein, Albert 16, 54
Eisenhower, Dwight 72
Engineering 32
Entertainment Merchant's Association 39
Escobar-Chavez, S. Liliana 125
Evil 30
Exxon Valdez 56

F

Faraday, Michael 54
Farmers 22, 23
FDA 70
Federal Government 9
Fifty Shades of Grey 91
Fitness Trainer 14
Fleming, Alexander 72
Fogelsville, PA 20
Football 36, 37

Foster, Jodie 129
Fox, Michael J. 74
Fracking 79
Frank, Anne 203
Franklin, Ben 15, 17, 57
Fruition Juice 25

G

G-Rated 12
Gambling 210
Garrison, William Loyd 87
GDP 159, 192
GED 172
Gehrig, Lou 19
Gel Electrophoresis 60
Gender Equality 32
Gettysburg 18
George Washington Bridge 36
Gifford, Kathie Lee 117
Girls 30, 32
Glover, John 58
GMO 70
Goodwin, Doris Kearns 54, 77
GRE 56, 165
Greene, Nathaniel 58

H

Hamilton, Alexander 13, 58, 89
Hedren, Tippi 116
Heroin 21
High Wild and Tight 8

Hill, Heather 64
Hobbes, Thomas 153
Hodges, Gil 137
Houk, Ralph 137
HPV 126
Hunting, Will 81

I

Independence Hall 153
Indian Wars 91
Industrial Revolution 9
Irving, Barrington 156
Ivy League 23
Ivy Tech 191

J

Jackson, Jesse 211
Jenner, Edward 71
Jersey City, NJ 61
Jobs, Steve 5
Jonathan Livingston Seagull 144
Jones, Angus 7
Jones, Lolo 108
Jungle, The 184

K

Keppler, Johannes 71
Khmer Rouge 88
King James Bible 55
King, Rodney 87

Knox, Henry 58
Kutcher, Ashton 118

L

Lab Work 18
Lambert, Lisa 17
Lawrence, Jennifer 126
Lennon, John 95
Lin, Jeremy 135
Lincoln, Abraham 54, 55, 85, 89
Little House on the Prairie 8, 111, 125, 126, 202
Little Round Top 18
Locke, John 153

M

Macon Georgia 38
Macon Mustangs 38
Mao, Chairman 66
Madonna 115
Mandela, Nelson 170
Martin, Billy 8
Martin, Dean 125
Martin, Trayvon 87
Matsui, Hideki 155
McCarthy, Jenny 77
McDonald's 40
Media 38
Mencken, H.L. 4
Mensa 56

Mepham High School 36
Mitosis 27
Montessori, Maria 54
Myelin 24

N

Napoleon 6
National Education Association 17
National Institutes of Health 124
National Parks System 69
National Vital Statistics 107
Nepotism 58
Nettles, Graig 10
Nerve Impulses 24
New Jersey 35
New York City 19, 186
New York Giants 211
Newark, NJ 61
Newton, Isaac 80
Nickelback 123, 124
No Child Left Behind 63
Nolte, Dorothy Law 190

O

Obama, Barack 76
Officer Candidate School 55
Oppenheimer, Robert 72
Oscars 57

P

Palin, Bristol 117
Parker, Kathleen 76
Parkinson's 40, 74
PBS 77
Pasteur, Louis 71, 140, 196
Payton, Walter 135
Pedagogy 4
P-Tech High School 173
Ph.D. 27
Philadelphia, PA 170
Philadelphia Eagles 211
Physical Education 97
Planned Parenthood 90
Poe, Edgar Allan 94
Polyploid 27
Pornography 35
Pot, Pol 66
Powell, Colin 88
Plumbers 22, 23
Prep School 18
Prison Rates 30
Private Schools 7
Provincetown MA 108
Public Schools 7

R

Race to the top 63
Rape 91
Red Book Magazine 129
Reece, Pee Wee 88
Reid, Richard 138
Remediation 59
Restriction Enzymes 61, 62
Reuters 40
Rhee, Michelle 187, 189
Rickey, Branch 211
Ripkin, Cal 134
Roberts, Cokie 77
Robinson, Jackie 86, 88, 211
Rockwell, Norman 197
Roe v. Wade 91
Roosevelt, Teddy 68, 69

S

Salk, Jonas 74, 76
Samuels, Christina 100
Sanders, Barry 134
Sandy Hook Elementary 39
SAT 32, 56, 165
Schizophrenia 40
School Choice 59
Scott-Clayton, Judith 179
Simple Machines 25
Saxum 20
Sex in the City 115
Shaw, George Bernard 176, 177
Shoe Bomber 138
Shock Jocks 31
Sinclair, Upton 184
Snow, Charles Percy 65
Socratic Method 14
Soldiers 58

Special Education 30, 101-104
Sperm Donors 120
Stalin, Joseph 66
STDs 124
Steinbeck, John 209
Stem Cells 75, 76
Stockholm Sweden 98
Stowe, Harriet Beecher 87
Suicide 35
Supreme Court 39

T

Team of Rivals 54
Tecumseh 193
Teresa, Mother 212
Thome, Jim 134
Three Springs Ministry 201
Tillman, Pat 138
Title X 90
Tocqueville, Alexis de 29
Townsend, Robert 163
TSA 197
Tyre, Peg 147

U

Underground Railroad 87
Unions 194
United States 80

V

Vacuum 30
Venezuela 80
Venice Beach 15
Videotaping 135
Vietnam 73
Voltaire 153

W

Wall Street Journal 63
Wang, Stephanie 179
Waltons, The 111, 125, 202
Washington, George 58, 73
Washington Post 17
West Point 156
Williams, Laura 37
Williams, Ted 137, 138
Wilson, Woodrow 208
Winehouse, Amy 116
Woodshop 4
World War II 72, 73, 137,
    138, 210
Wrestlers 31
Wright Brothers 67
Wulf, William 27